Speak The Unspoken

Exploring the Unwritten Rules of North Norway

Gabriela Sirbu

Migration of Emotion

Speak The Unspoken
Exploring the Unwritten Rules of North Norway

Published by
Migration of Emotion

Tromsø, Norway

www.migrationofemotion.com

Copyright © 2022 *by Gabriela Sirbu*

Cover Design by Alyssa Noelle Coelho of Lionheart Creations

Interior Design by Dawn Teagarden

ISBN (e-book): 978-82-692962-0-4

ISBN: (paperback) 978-82-692962-1-1

To My Father

Contents

Part 3 - Holidays

Author's Note

As an immigrant to North Norway, I found it difficult to understand the values which govern people's everyday lives here. They are very different from the values I grew up with and, generally, different from the values in other western countries according to what I hear while speaking to other immigrants, or reading books or blogs written by other immigrants or listening to podcasts.

The challenge is that many of these *values are unwritten.* If we are lucky, Norwegian friends tell us about them, or teachers might mention them in Norwegian culture classes. At the same time, even if we are told about them, it is difficult to completely change our behavior and brush away the years experienced in our cultures of origin. Our Norwegian helpers explain the best they can about the things which happen in their country, but they explain them with the experience of being born and raised in Norway.

This book is about some of these unwritten rules and differences, from an immigrant's point of view. I hope that my shared experiences will help other ex-pats established in North Norway. The stories are *personal,* and the interpretations of the events are *subjective.* Another thing I need to mention is that I live and have always lived in North Norway, and I am told that the culture here is different from the one in the South of Norway. Therefore, my stories are primarily influenced by North Norwegian culture. I am also aware that what I am presenting here is only a scratch on the surface of a very complex culture and people.

I am presenting some *perspectives* that unfolded as the light shined upon them in my adjustment. As you read, think about *your own experience* as an immigrant as well. The *two perspectives combined* may give you an even better picture, maybe closer to *your truth.*

May this book be of use to those who read it!

Gabriela Sirbu

Part 1

Working Life

Hard Skills vs. Soft Skills

One of the issues I see many foreigners dealing with when they come to North Norway is the value of the degree(s) they bring with them from their country of origin. Degrees and qualifications obtained through formal education and/or working experience are called "hard skills." I'm sure you've heard this term.

First, the diploma/degree needs to be recognized by NOKUT.no; however, that is not always a guarantee that it will help you get a job related to that degree. Some degrees are not recognized in Norway, and it is difficult to use them if they are. One of these is Law. When you study Law, you learn the law of your country of origin, not the Norwegian Law, which is very difficult to understand and interpret even for Norwegians who speak the language. Most foreigners I know who are practicing law in Norway have studied it in

Norway or have studied International Law and work for companies with activities all over the world. I know quite a few people from many countries with a law degree who are doing completely different work because of this.

Another degree would be in History. Usually, history teachers are learning the history of their own country and not Norwegian history. Teaching is not even the same in Norway. There are teachers for exact science (realfag) where you're supposed to cover almost all exact sciences from math to chemistry, biology, and physics; and there are "samfunnsfag" teachers who are supposed to cover everything in social sciences from history to religion and foreign languages.

The important detail in looking for work in North Norway is your personality and demonstrating that you are willing to adjust and do what is needed. The willingness to contribute to Norwegian society and play your part is called a "soft skill."

If you need a job, references are the key— and not just any references. I recommend having Norwegian references. People tend to trust their kind more. When I say "their kind," I mean either a Norwegian or a foreigner that has been here for a long time and is well-integrated and speaks the language very well. You can get references by doing volunteer work. Generally, in Norway, there is a volunteering culture (dugnad): organizing festivals, arrangements, dinners for the poor, answering crisis phone calls, organizing sports events and tournaments, selling stuff to support clubs, etc. Actions and completed work count just as much as the relationships you build together with people you volunteer for and the other volunteers on the site. Also important are the experiences you have gathered doing things with others on a team that serves a higher purpose than the personal ones. If there are people interested in results in that group, and you manage to bring those, that matters, too. At the same time, remember that you didn't manage to bring the results on your own—you were part of a team, and the team matters.

If you need money quickly, then you may want to set your degree aside. Try to get a job in tourism, restaurant business, cleaning, logistics, kindergarten, etc. These are the most available ones if you do not speak the language yet. In the end, they count, because they put a roof over your head and food on the table fast. They also offer a place where you can show *who you are* and where you can build relationships that can provide good references.

If you have a roof over your head, food on the table, and money is not needed so fast, then you can use some time to find something that suits you and/or the education that formed you. Yet keep in mind that if you have experience from your culture, it may not be useful if it is not familiar to the people you show it to. It means that you need to find similar references and ways to describe it in your new culture, so people can understand what you have been doing and what you do well.

Living in Northern Norway for nearly twenty years, I have been using plenty of skills that I have learned in my country of origin while working as a journalist. But I realized I had to adjust to this country and its people. What worked back there does not necessarily work here. For my part, the skill that I used the most was the ability to be curious and to listen—to listen more than talk. Nevertheless, I saw it as essential to talk, and especially to be entertaining. People will always love a "clown," yet some funny jokes in your own country and language may not be as funny in Norway. Humor is special to each culture, and it needs to be handled with care. If not, it can send the wrong signals.

It is all about interpretation and translation; and in my view, it is also about diversity. It is not about being "better," but being "different." It would be best if you express how we are different and how that difference can contribute to the new company/community. Unfortunately, we, as human beings, tend to run away from diversity because it implies change; and we like familiarity more than what is unknown, and more than we would like to admit.

In addition to handling diversity with care, the willingness and the ability to learn are just as important. The fact that you have been doing various jobs also shows that you are not afraid to get your hands dirty. If you are a man, for instance, and you are not willing to help with the cleaning chores in the shared break rooms, making coffee, and even cooking sometimes, you may not be very successful. Norway generally is strong when it comes to gender equality, and women know their rights. Women are also in charge many times, and it is important to make a good impression. In the same way, if you are a woman and you do not help with snow shoveling or carpentry tasks or changing car tires, again, you may want to reconsider. There are many tools now that have made this work easy for women to do as well.

Remember that your personality, your ability to adjust, to speak for yourself, and to treat people well are part of who you are. They are your "soft skills"; and, many times, they matter more than your diplomas or "hard skills".

My questions for you now are:

- How significant is your degree for you?

- In case you need to, are you willing to set it aside and start all over?

- Did you study because you liked the subjects, or just because your family wanted you to do it? Or only because your friends learned the same thing?

- How much studying was a decision that came from your heart and how much was imposed on you by your family/society?

If you ended up with a degree in a subject you don't like, now is your chance to start over and try different things so you can find out what you like/want.

What's a Hobby Good For?

If you already live in Norway, perhaps you have heard the expression "Norwegians work to live; they do not live to work." True in some measure, there are many Norwegians who define themselves by their jobs; and if they don't have one, they can meet the stigma from society. There are also few Norwegians who work a lot, on weekends too, enjoy what they do, and do not consider work to be a chore. An old teacher of mine once told me, "Gabriela, if you like what you do, you do not work one day in your life." I am experiencing those words, and I enjoy the process.

At the same time, for those who have jobs, it is also important to have so-called "leisure time activities" or, in other words, hobbies.

The reason I have chosen to discuss hobbies is that every time I hold a course about job searching and I advise people to put their hobbies or interests in their CVs, I am met with surprised faces.

Most of the people who look surprised come from cultures where personal interests or problems are not brought up at work—where the employer is not interested in the private life of the employees. The only thing that matters is how the employees can be more productive and how they can bring more money and more results to the company, usually requiring unpaid overtime.

In Norway generally, if your leader or your colleagues see you working overtime, it is possible that they may not like it. That is a sign that you do not have a personal life. Perhaps your intention is to show how devoted you are to the company, yet the company does not need overworked people who do not know their own limits when it comes to being tired. Being tired is the first sign of illness.

Therefore, it is important to have a hobby. Your colleagues from your work and/or future employer are interested in what you like to do in your spare time. Your hobby may be the key to participating in the "water cooler" or coffee breaks and lunch conversations. This way, the employer knows if you will fit in the team or if you'll have subjects to talk about with your colleagues, or if your hobby may happen to be the same as a task in your job. If that is a coincidence, then your motivation will be secured. You'll be working out of pleasure, you'll get energy out of your work, and you'll enjoy your workplace. It will be a win-win both for the company and for you. Imagine how it would be to be paid for working on your hobby, without having to go through the hustle of running a business based on your hobby.

Being in Norway (just as in any other country), there are some subjects and hobbies that one may be more careful about: politics, money, and religion. It may be better to stick with the "safe" hobbies like cooking, knitting, car repairing, carpentry, sound/video editing, any kind of sports both outdoor and indoor, books, music, and even dancing. If you play an instrument, make sure that you can play pop music on it also; classical music may not be everyone's cup of tea. Traveling, painting and drawing, computer/TV games, and arranging parties are also safe. This one comes in handy if the company needs someone to arrange Christmas or summer parties. This used to be my hobby. Now, I make parties on Zoom with totally different themes. Socializing and volunteering can also be a hobby. Singing in a choir is popular. There are also jumping parachutes, paragliding, etc.

Having things to do in your spare time tells people around you who you are as a person and how you can participate in the social life of your company or your neighborhood. Common interests are more likely to help you acquire friends, more than anything else. Therefore, write your hobbies in your CV and talk about them in the lunchroom. It can pay off.

If you do not have a hobby, or if you do not know what you like, perhaps it would be a good idea for you to think about what it is that you really enjoy doing in your spare time. Or, if it were not for the money, how would you like to spend your time?

Attitudes and Job Interviews

Some time ago, I went to a seminar on how to get the best candidates to apply for jobs. The seminar was held by two prominent headhunting Norwegian companies.

The information shared was about writing a job ad and how to best describe what you can offer as a company. It was also about what a company requires from a future employee. Fair enough. There were about one hundred people in the room and almost all of them had team responsibilities in their organizations.

At a certain point, one of the presenters delivered a quiz with two questions which drew my attention. One was asking how long it takes interviewers to form an impression about the person they interview before deciding if they will hire the candidate or not: 25 minutes, 8 minutes, or 4 minutes. The entire room raised their hands for the "4 minutes" answer. There were also comments from the audience about hand-shaking, body language, smiling, eye contact, and other details which can determine how good a first impression can be made.

The second interesting question was about personality type. This seems to be most important in a first-round interview and what people see at a first meeting: extroversion, conscientiousness, work ethic, or agreeableness. Again, the entire room voted for "agreeableness."

It was the most important thing almost everybody in the audience seemed to agree upon. This makes me think that being a pleasant person might be just as important as if you do a good job or not. The important thing is not to make your colleagues feel inadequate, uncomfortable, or stupid, for that matter. The last ones can easily be done by being hard-working, outspoken, or even by having good ideas. I am not saying that one shouldn't be hard-working or speak out if one has good ideas. I am saying that one should be careful about *how* they present themselves when doing so. The attitude one has when presenting a new idea is sometimes more important than the idea itself.

"Gut" feeling plays a big role in the society we live in. Maybe this plays a bigger part here than in any other country in the world. Even though, in my experience, people do not seem to be very aware of how "emotional" decisions are being taken in their business, they just act on it. Many haven't yet heard about Daniel Kahneman who won the Nobel prize in economics in 2002 with the proven theory that people buy things based on emotions. It's not a stretch to assume that the decision about who they hire is also emotionally-based to a large degree.

I have met quite a few hard-working people, engaged and motivated, but struggling to find jobs, mostly because they do not know that their strong and outgoing personalities may appear frightening or threatening to our countrymen.

Perhaps those of you who went to interviews in North Norway noticed the personality questions you were asked. They sound like: "What are your positive sides or negative sides?" or "Do you think there is anything you could improve?" These are questions difficult to answer for people coming from abroad. Firstly, because positive and negative sides may be two sides of the same sharp knife. If this is the case, make a list of everything you think or you know that you are good at. Then, on the same piece of paper, write down the opposite of those qualities. Those represent your opportunity for improving potential. If you speak about them in an interview, it will show that you know yourself. It indicates that you are not perfect and you would like to develop yourself within the company interviewing you. It will also show that you are aware of other opportunities given to you by the company, which don't always come as a paycheck. This will show your motivation beyond the financial benefits.

Moreover, something that overqualified people unable to find jobs in North Norway stumble over is *confidence*. The confidence one may feel inside will shine outside as *overconfidence*. It is natural, considering that when one is called in for an interview, one wants to make a great first impression and, as a result, they can overreact in a meeting. In this way, the distance between *overconfidence* and *arrogance* can be a very small step. This type of attitude is not something that people like in North Norway. Check online the Law of Jante, which I am not writing about in this book, assuming that many people know about it already. If you don't, check it out by registering for my newsletter:

https://migrationofemotion.simplero.com/page/144171

Some of you may say, "Yes, but Norwegians can be arrogant themselves." It might be true for some, as it is true for many people in other countries. As the saying tells us: "People usually do not see the bar in their own eyes, but they see the stick in the others." It is a form of common sense and common knowledge as old as Jesus, one which we call "human nature."

How do we explain this to people from countries where qualities such as confidence, self-assurance, boldness, and outspokenness are required in their work markets? How easy is it for these people to change their behavior in order to fit into this new, "emotional" yet "cold" society?

And more importantly, are people willing to change their behavior? Would they think it is worth it to change who they think they are so they would be accepted in the new environment? Do they wish to work together with someone else who might be able to help them, like a coach or someone who knows how to explain the culture with words?

Leadership by Coffee Cup

There are leaders, and there are bosses. It is a known concept in leadership training. In my country of origin, I experienced many types of "bosses." These people walk in and give instructions; nobody dares to speak to them, and they have a beautiful secretary who makes coffee. The "boss" brings an expensive car into the work parking lot and the same day an announcement is made about a delay in salary payments. They never have time to speak with their employees; and, if they do, it is to shout at them. I had these experiences a long time ago, in my birth country and judging by what I currently see in the news or when I travel back there, it doesn't seem like things have changed much.

In Norway, I discovered a kind of leadership very different from the authoritarian type I had experienced in my country of birth. I explored many reasons for this when I took a project management module at university. I enjoy following various courses and peeking into other areas of expertise to try to understand different worlds. I think it has to do with my background in journalism. It also helped me improve my Norwegian vocabulary, and it developed my knowledge of the language over the years.

During the project management class, I came across an interesting phrase: "Leadership by coffee cup." This expression puts into words what I've seen over the years of work and life in Norway. Unlike "bosses," the leader walks around the office or schedules meetings to talk to people in his/her team over a cup of coffee. Now, this ideal is not met everywhere, but it stands as a general circumstance. The most common thing known as "working form" in Norway is "the meeting." Another rule is the "open-door policy." The office door is open, so it is easy to go and speak to your superior about any queries you might have.

It is also believed that a friendly and understanding leader keeps the team together and productive, even for a modest salary. I have met people who would rather be paid less and work for someone kind and generous than work for a higher salary with a less sympathetic leader.

During my working life in North Norway, I've had superiors that made coffee for us, drove us wherever we needed to be as a team or to do our job, made dinner for us, and took time to listen to our issues. Maybe our problems weren't always fixable, but the simple fact that we could talk about them played a big part in keeping us motivated and together.

I have also met leaders who listened and displayed no facial expressions. You know there will be no compassion from them as they're only talking to you because it is expected of them. If politics promote friendly leadership, it doesn't mean all the leaders can and will be friendly. After a while, you stop wanting to talk to them and find yourself looking for another job.

When it comes to department leaders, the culture is that they have to be friendly with everybody, from their right-hand people to the cleaning personnel. At the same time, they will seldomly step over the lines of responsibility between departments or break the hierarchy.

For instance, I have a friend who used to work in a hotel. One day, he was having a friendly chat with his senior manager, enjoying a level of familiarity he was not used to. Half an hour later, he received a phone call from his direct supervisor, asking him to pe form a task. He instinctively knew that the senior manager must have contacted his supervisor. My friend was furious. He could not understand why the senior manager had not spoken with him directly. I realized that familiarity and friendly nature could be difficult to understand for foreigners, as friendliness does not always apply within the organizational hierarchy.

I suspected the senior manager wanted to respect the supervisor's role, so he preferred not to overstep the mark; the supervisor knows his team much better and can give direct feedback to each person accordingly. When I explained that to my friend, I realized that even though Norway projects the idea of equality, there remains the organizational hierarchy that needs to be respected. Otherwise, the natural "order" of things is ruined. This is something no one is trained in when they start a new job. People are trained on how to do the work tasks, but not in "work environment law" which states all this hierarchy. Not even Norwegian people get trained in this. Yet, they know it because they are born and raised here. It is natural for them. People get knowledge about work environment law from the Unions, or by taking extra roles inside the company, like being "tillitsvalgt," which is the representative of the Union at the workplace. Another role would be "verneombud," which is supposed to be like an extended hand of the leadership among the employees, and they are supposed to make sure that the leader does the job according to the law. In many companies though, this "verneombud" role is only responsible for safety at the workplace (HMS), like checking to make sure the employees' health is not at risk in their workplace from bad ventilation, dysfunctional machines, toxicity in labs, and screen pollution, poor body posture, air quality, noise, etc. Mental health, however, is not considered. It is still a taboo subject.

As immigrants, we have little chance of understanding all this structure if it is not explained to us in detail. Therefore, my friend didn't know it; and I didn't know it either, even though I was already living here for quite some time. The explanation I gave at the time was what I thought was reasonable, so it could help my friend. Later, after I took a role as "verneombud" in the organization I was working for, I found out that I was right.

Dare to Speak Up, or Don't

I work with people—people who struggle with cultural differences and who do not know how to approach their team leaders or employers, as they have their own perceptions of good reasons to approach a boss.

I know that in many countries, "the boss" might equate with "God" in the work environment, and people do not dare to speak in front of him or her. This can even be the case in situations when they face challenges at work and they could use some guidance or support. It is something that some people find hard to do. People cannot imagine speaking with their employer about their private and personal life; in situations when they are sick,have difficulties in marriage, are dealing with a sick child or family member, or when they experience a challenge. In some work environments in other countries, people can lose their jobs by mentioning such "frivolities" to their boss.

Yet, for Norwegians, this is a natural and logical thing to do. In my experience in this country (almost two decades), "bosses" or "leaders" have their roles. They are motivators and consultants when they are needed. Even if they may not know how to help you, they will listen and find a solution together with you. Many times, speaking with the person responsible for your work about the things which bother you can be helpful.

First, it removes the feeling of guilt—guilt for not being good enough, or not productive enough. Once you tell your boss and he or she knows about it, the burden is shared and it helps dissipate a big part of the stress accumulated in your body. Eliminating the stress is a huge help, and then you might notice that you find the solution to your problem on your own. If necessary, the boss can come with suggestions and helpful guidance. The only condition here is to put the issue on the table in a constructive and friendly way. You are all in it together, and speaking about it helps because it's in the team's interest to know, too. It is a sign that you can handle stress, that you know your limits, that you know yourself, and that you are able to ask for help, which are all signs of maturity.

Similarly, this applies when you have personal problems. You are not doing your company or your boss any favors by having "reduced" productivity caused by something that happens in your private life. Talking about it (in a private meeting you ask for) helps them to see the bigger picture better. You only see your own corner, while they know that for a time you might be distracted or absent for good reasons and can find help for you and your colleagues.

This system works in Norway because we live in an egalitarian society, and it is expected of you to share and participate. You do your share, participating when you also volunteer for new tasks, and show that you are interested. At the same time, you participate and do your share when you say "no" to something because you cannot do it.

Norwegians are encouraged to think for themselves and to find their own way of solving a work task. They don't receive many guidelines and are expected to figure things out themselves, which can be a challenge for people who come from societies where they are used to being told what to do. They are also expected to figure out what they have to do and this can be difficult when you don't know that this is a cultural mark in the work environment.

The Trust-Based Society

There is also another concept in Norwegian working life, called "frihet under ansvar." It can be translated word by word to "freedom under responsibility" or, maybe better, "the freedom of responsibility," or... I am sure there is an even better way of putting it.

The concept has to do with the fact that, generally, people are hired to do a job but they don't have anyone over their shoulder to control them or to "whip" them to get the job done. This freedom is essential, especially because in Norway, family life and free time are significant values (despite the divorce rate and the increase in the number of single-parent households). When you have kids to pick up from kindergarten or school by 16:00 at the latest, of course, you go and pick them up, even if you haven't finished your work. But when the family dinner is over and the children are in bed, many people continue to work from home in order to complete what they need to by the next day.

It is the same with doctor appointments and even hairdresser appointments, or if you are waiting for the plumber or the electrician to come to fix something at your house, or you need to take your car to the garage. These services are offered in many towns only until 16:00. In Norway, in theory and action, everybody must be treated the same, have the same working hours if possible, and enjoy family or leisure time at the same hours. If so, you let your closest superior or your colleagues know that you need to get somewhere—over a cup of coffee, or send them an email, or call, or text—and then you take time from work and go do your thing.

People are trusted that they are doing their jobs, and this trust and freedom create very good results in many workplaces. The burden and the stress of not being able to speak to your leader are removed. It is easier to accomplish your tasks in a stress-free environment than in a stressful one. Many leaders understand that their team has enough to cope with while doing the work; people do not need an extra stress factor, not from the leader.

The language used by leaders is also unique in itself. I never heard anyone "commanding" or "ordering" me to do something. I've mostly heard phrases like "I think you almost need to do..." or "Perhaps we should do ..." or "Is there anyone who could have available time to ..." when the meaning behind it is actually "You/the team *have to* do this...." If it goes so far that they need to use direct and sharp expressions, then it is not pleasant for them. Most of the time, I like this politeness spoken with calm tones. It is what Eirin Meyer, in *The Culture Map,* calls a "high context society"—one in which we're supposed to read between the lines. Yet, what almost nobody speaks about out loud is that reading between the lines is also a skill that people developed while being born and raised in this society. It is especially difficult to learn when you come from a culture that is more direct or authoritarian.

The criticism is also carefully given. After enumerating all the positive things about your or the team's work, you might hear something about areas that need improvement. Personally, I have had trouble with positive feedback and then hearing the well-hidden criticism. On second thought, this way of giving feedback, dressed in a sweet, positive coat, only makes the discussion and the time spent together nicer. Yet, it is difficult to understand this way of communicating when you come from a culture where you first hear about the things you don't do well at your job.

I have also met ex-pats placed in positions of leadership in a Norwegian organization who became perceived as less accessible because this is not natural to them. Many Norwegians do not like the sharp way of speaking and giving directions, and they have their way of showing that. One way would be to take sick leave. Another would be to refuse or not "have time" to do the tasks. Another efficient way of protesting is speaking behind the leader's back so they may not have the next advancing opportunity so easy coming.

I think this happens in many countries: conspiring, office politics behind leaders' backs, gossip, judgments, etc. It is not invented in Norway; yet, it takes far less to stir waters as people here are far more sensitive than in other countries. For good reasons, we are all the result of the historical and social context; and Norway has had many years of welfare—welfare which gave time to people to refine their sensitivity.

The Clash of Meeting Cultures

I am probably not the only person who speaks about *Norwegian meeting culture*. It is very difficult to understand for many foreigners. I also struggled with it for many years, until I decided to just befriend it. And suddenly, I understood how it worked.

Many immigrants are coming from cultures where "time is money" and the use of time needs to be efficient and produce results— visible results. People's time is not supposed to be "wasted" by being called into meetings where they are not necessarily needed.

When they come to Norway and they start working, they notice that there is a lot of time spent in meetings, where many people sit together and talk calmly. Everyone who has something to say, *and dares to say it*, speaks and states their opinions, or misunderstanding, confusion, or frustrations. All the others are listening politely, and nobody speaks out of turn or above someone who is already speaking. In Norwegian, there is an expression: "å snakke i munnen på hverandre." It is one that is used for people who do not have the patience to hear the whole argument of someone who is already speaking and try to hurry it along by interrupting. Translated word by word, it is "to speak in each other's mouths without listening." This is something that is looked upon as being typically foreign and rude. I also find in this society a bigger sense of "listening to understand" rather than "listening to answer" (Steven Covey). In my understanding, the first one implies a bigger measure of curiosity and compassion while the second one implies a sense of "smartness," which in my opinion is not always smart. Yet, it is a method of protection that people coming from societies with hot blood carry with them. The faster the answers and the arguments are coming, the "smarter" one is. Yet in Norway, that attitude can be considered rude.

As I mentioned, some of these meetings, at first sight, do not seem to have any productive end. There is no result visible. At the same time, they are important, because the people participating in them need to speak out loud whatever they have in their hearts regarding the topics on the agenda. Speaking out loud together with others is part of the productive process. This is how people get ideas from each other, and this is how they progress together. It is also the way people get to know each other and eventually build relationships and comradery. There is also a saying that goes something like "If you want to go fast, walk alone. If you want to go far, walk together with others." I don't know who said it, yet I find it fits well in the Norwegian culture. It is important that people walk on a path together, in teams. This is also the slogan of the Norwegian Labor Party: "Alle skal med," which means "Nobody is left out," Of course, nothing is perfect; therefore, Norwegian society has its "left outs" even if it is not the intention.

Over time, I have also noticed that people are "invited" to meetings and not necessarily "ordered" to be in them, as it can be the habit in other cultures. When they hear the word "invitation to a meeting," many foreigners in Norway have a tendency to dismiss it, because "invitation" means that there is a possibility of choosing if one wants to go or not. Participation is not "mandatory."

Well, from a Norwegian point of view, participation *is* mandatory. If someone took the time to consider that you should be invited to a meeting, it means that they want to include you in the process. It means that those people are given a chance to be present and to participate, learn, and eventually, contribute to the process.

It may be that you're attending the meeting and not saying anything, but your simple presence can influence a lot. You never know how another person in the room can get a good idea just by looking at you, or just by knowing that you are there. If you do not attend, it can send signals that you are not interested and that you do not care about the work your colleagues are doing, and yourself as well, since you are part of the team. It can also signal a lack of respect.

As I said earlier, these meetings are the "working method" in Norway. Attending them can be very useful and you can get a lot of information from them—information that perhaps wouldn't come out in any other setting except that meeting. It is also a way to learn how people speak and how they present arguments. You may notice that some are better speakers and some are better arguers than others.

The speech and meeting culture has a long tradition in Norway. Pretty much everyone knows how to hold a speech or how to speak in a meeting because they have been doing it since they were children. All family gatherings, baptisms, weddings, confirmations, round year birthday celebrations include speeches from various persons. Even in restaurants, the waiter is presenting, in a speech, the menu for the evening. Some children also choose activities in school which allow them to develop this skill. If you have kids in school, it can be a good idea to guide them to go places where they learn to speak in public.

Of course, when you have an opinion that you state loudly, you should expect feedback as well; and learning how to deal with that is another issue. This is, again, different from culture to culture.

For many foreigners though, this way of interacting in meetings is either unknown or associated with bad experiences, especially if, in their culture of origin, a meeting meant being criticized or publicly humiliated. In some cultures, these are "motivational" methods.

These types of meetings are known for people who experienced severe regimes, or simply just societies with *result-oriented* cultures where people are not important except if they are producing something. Therefore, doing too much or more than is expected can sometimes be experienced as "off-putting" in a Norwegian context.

As I see it, Norwegian culture is more *relationship and network-oriented*. How well people in a team get along is more important than the result. *BEING* can be more important than *DOING* in certain contexts. The result comes when the time is right.

Therefore, my suggestion is to become friends with the meetings you are invited to and go to all of them. Give people who invited you the possibility to get used to your presence, and also your contributing ideas.

WHY Should You Join a Union While in Norway?

I work with people who are immigrants in Norway. Some of them have issues with their employers; yet every time I ask if they are members of a Union, I receive frightened and confused looks in return.

I understand that in many other countries, being a member of a Union can be too good to be true. In Norway, though, it has more advantages than disadvantages. I remember telling this to a friend of mine who does not live in Norway. She replied, "In my company, we were already warned that if we join a Union, we're going to lose our jobs. So, this is not something I can do, because I need my job." We all need our jobs, for various reasons.

When it comes to Unions in Norway, they are well-organized. However, there are many, and you need to find the right one representing the people's interests in your field of work.

Here are some of the advantages of unions:

1. The money you pay for a membership can be considered nondeductible income, which means it is money you do not pay tax on.

2. Every time there are salary negotiations for your working field, the Union negotiates for you as well, even if you didn't ask for it personally. They will negotiate in the name of all their members. Usually, each Union sends a warning to its members about what they need to do in good time before the negotiations start.

3. If you experience injustices at your workplace, you can speak to people from the Union, get advice and make a plan so you can make yourself heard. They accompany you in the meetings and even speak for you if necessary. They also have lawyers who can offer legal aid. Most of the conflicts at work are solved by the Unions.

4. They can negotiate better house mortgage interests for their members.

5. Many negotiate good deals for all sorts of insurances, from house to car and even hotel and rental.

6. They sometimes assist with scholarships for education.

7. They sometimes provide courses and conferences in your field of work so you can keep yourself updated. For those, the employer usually gives time off from work and sometimes even pays for them.

8. The network meetings and events help you get to know your colleagues and most of these events are free of charge for members.

9. You get information about things happening inside your field of work through a magazine or regular emails. It's good to know what's happening around you.

10. If you want to get involved, you can become a representative yourself and help. It is a good opportunity for learning inside this kind of organization. It is a job that you're not paid for; it is like volunteering inside your working place. But for that, your employer gives you the time off so

you can work with it. You're not paid in money, but in time. In return, you learn something new, meet new people, grow your network, and contribute to your colleague's work welfare and your own.

11. If you are a student or are unemployed, the membership fee is lower, and the information you get is helpful and keeps you updated with news on the work market.

From what I hear from people I work with, some of the skepticism towards Unions comes from their experiences in their countries of origin. Other reasons would be that many of them do not work full-time, but for a couple of months in a raw, seasonal type of work, and then they travel back to their own country. Others simply do not know that something like this exists, what it is, and what it is good for. Of course, not learning the language is also a disadvantage. If one does not speak even English, it isn't easy to find out about this kind of thing, and one has to depend on his or her own compatriots to get information and help. They can only help you as far as they have come themselves.

If you already are a member of a Union, I suggest acquainting yourself with the person elected as your representative in your department. Find out more about how they can help you and how you can help them. After all, they work for you, too.

If you have not joined a Union yet, my suggestion would be to find out which one can represent people in your work field best. Find their website, read the information there, give them a call, and join. You won't regret it.

The Concept of "Time"
in North Norway

The concept of "time" is very different in North Norway compared to South Norway (so I am told) and other countries I have visited. Again, some of this is my experience and my subjective perception of it. I grew up with the idea that one should do things quickly, almost without thinking properly, because everything needed to be done yesterday. My experience prior to my life in the North taught me that "time flies." I grew up thinking that time passed very quickly, and it needed to be used before it did.

I heard the same thing from friends living in other parts of the world and in countries I visited: "get ahead quickly," "make money quickly," and "climb up the ladder as fast as possible," "get married quickly," "have children quickly." Life is short and one wants to make the most of it. The older you grow, the feeling that your life is slipping away through youɪ ....ᵍ gets more and more intense.

Not in the part of Norway I live in, I thought. Here time "comes" and it never "goes." I struggled to understand this idea during my first years here, but someone old and wise explained it to me. The context was about the indigenous people in North Norway— the Saami people. If a Saami person says he or she will pay you a visit, they put it like this: "I'll be visiting today. And if I don't visit you today, I will do it tomorrow. And if I don't come to visit tomorrow, I will come another day." In other words, the promised visit will happen when the time feels right for the person visiting.

It's true that we've heard this in other cultures as well, but here it has its own meaning, and I think it relates somehow to welfare. Although neither the Saami people nor the Norwegian people were rich until 1969, they had—and still have—more than us, a stronger sense of *"enjoying the journey"* than *"reaching a goal."*

"Feeling" what happens in the process of reaching a goal, and the experience gathered, are more important than the accomplishment of the goal. There is a saying in Norwegian, which sounds like "The path becomes while we're walking" because people learn from the experience they gather. You cannot know how to reach a goal until you are there, and you have the experience of it. Therefore, it feels like reaching a goal just happens. It seems, from the outside, that it was never planned, even though public organizations and private companies have strategic plans. Time is used as a tool in the process, and I often hear the expression "we want to have a good time." The good time is used for brainstorming and for new ideas to grow on people. Simultaneously, this time is also used for people to have room and space to deal with the feelings which may occur during the processes. It seems to me that even though I hear that Norway is characterized as being a "cold" nation, many feelings are "boiling" behind the icy appearance. It is just that they learned not to let them show in public, or to people they don't know. This is why time is needed. To let the boiling cool, before feedback or bad news is given.

It takes a lot of time to get to know a Norwegian as they don't trust strangers easily, even if the predominant politics were, until recently, very tolerant in this sense. But between the political platforms and the woman selling shoes or food in a shop, or the farmer working the land above the Polar Circle, it is a very long way. It is a distance measured just as much in time, as it is in kilometers. There is a big difference between what politicians say and what normal people do at home, in small towns and villages.

The decision-making process is slower here. I thought I was a person who made decisions quickly, and I lived with that idea for many years. Living and working in this part of Norway made me realize that I was not quick; I was just running away from "feeling" the process of making a decision. Once, I had something that people call an "aha" moment when a colleague asked me to help with a project. In my head, everything about my work was planned and I knew I would not have the time required. And yet, a voice inside me told me to answer with, "Let me think about it." A part of me wanted to let him know as soon as possible that I could not help, and it pained me not to say anything until the next day when I was supposed to give him the answer. Putting myself in his shoes, I realized that I would have liked to get a quick answer, so I could move forward and find someone else to help me meet my deadline. That was because I like "making" things happen instead of depending on other people's help or answers. But, that was me. The next day, I gave my colleague the negative answer and, to my surprise, he wasn't as upset as I expected him to be. His answer was, "That's okay, I appreciate you taking the time to consider it." He then told me, "I must say that it might have been upsetting for me if you would have answered yesterday when I asked you. I would have taken it personally because you didn't even bother to think about it."

That was an interesting discovery. Until then, I didn't realize that even if there were deadlines and penalties at stake, one could still take it personally if you answered too quickly. It would have felt like a blunt and harsh rejection. He was not worried about the deadline or the penalties because there were no real consequences to him personally or even to the workplace. He was not going to lose anything or have his salary cut down. The time I used to think about my answer created a buffer, so he could take the rejection easier, and helped both of us to keep the good relationship.

I did not know all this then, nor did I understand the system at the time. I had my ideas and emotions about a "system," which I brought with me from my birth country. My "feelings" migrated together with me, and I brought to my new country my perception of time: Time "goes" instead of "comes."

Have you ever thought about how you react when you don't manage to get things done as quickly as you want, or as they are requested from you? Do you lose your temper or become irritated, or do you just find something else to do while you are waiting for things to happen? What works best for you?

This detail can be important to know about yourself, especially when it comes to dealing with authorities. The paperwork needed if you want to settle (i.e. security number, visa, work contracts) can take a lot of time. Yet bureaucracy around immigration processes is something in and of itself in many countries. This would not be different in Norway.

Part 2

Daily Life - Social Life

What Do We Have in Common with the Norwegians?

O r with any country we live in that is not our own? We have the present in common. We do not share their culture nor their past, two important aspects that reflect on the present. However, we share or they share with us, the same work market. We share stores, cinemas, streets, libraries, concert experiences, transportation, and restaurants.

A couple of years ago, I went to a meeting where the theme was children films and the voices used to dub the originals. A prominent figure in the field was speaking and some of the voices came to life right there. I noticed among my Norwegian peers how they recognized the characters and how their bodies leaned forward with excitement as they recalled voices and stories from their childhood.

I did not share the same excitement, but I remembered the films that had guided me through the labyrinth of learning the language. When I first started learning Norwegian, I used to watch a lot of children's films and TV channels, as they used a more simplified language than adults in everyday life. They were a huge help to me at the time. And yet, I did not have the same experience as my Norwegian peers who had watched them in their childhood. Their experience was linked to a happy memory while mine brought back a memory I could call painful at the time.

We do not know their history. It doesn't mean that all Norwegians know it, but they don't need to; it is in their blood. A condition for obtaining the right to live and to work in Norway is that one needs to take some hours of Norwegian history and civilization. I took the classes and passed the exam, but it doesn't mean that I remember all of it.

We don't know much about how they grew up nor their family history. We do not share a common understanding of our surroundings. We learn the rules of the social system we live in, as it is so much better than the system we'd left behind. Equally though, they don't know much about the countries we come from nor about our backgrounds or family history. As a newcomer, it is normal to experience skepticism. If you take a moment to think about it, are you comfortable with every new person you meet?

At one of my workplaces, we used to take a daily quiz at lunchtime. I could only answer a few questions; those about folk and pop music, history, or geography. Norway is a big and long country with many islands, fjords and valleys, each of them having local names just like in any other country. I could not answer questions about Norwegian film history, famous actors or singers or comedians, nor about historical figures or politicians, in any domain. However, I could answer questions about their classical music and literature, or European classical music and literature, since I had studied these topics at school behind the Iron Curtain during the Cold War. It is funny how we had to learn all sorts of things about all the countries in the world, yet we weren't allowed to travel and see them for ourselves.

To revisit my question about the things we have in common with the Norwegians, the answer is pretty clear. We have what we make of today, in the present moment. We have the language that we might or might not speak. (Some of the 500,000 immigrants living here don't even speak Norwegian.) We have the food we may share sometimes, the sun, and the unstable weather. Sometimes we have common interests and hobbies, and our children might go to the same schools. Only they will share the same experiences, teachers, birthday parties, friendships, and history, and they will speak the language just as well as the natives. They are the second-generation immigrants. They may feel at times embarrassed by the accent their parents have, or if one parent does not speak Norwegian yet. Perhaps they will be embarrassed to invite friends at home because of that and because they are trying so badly to be accepted.

Being an immigrant has so many more layers than speaking the language.

Speak the Words, Not the Culture

Learning Norwegian was difficult. It still is. At the beginning, listening to the sound of it reminded me of a stone avalanche, thousands of big and small rocks falling down a mountain. I realized that it would not be easy to learn.

I took evening classes and spent many hours memorizing words, irregular verbs, and expressions that change meaning with the context they are used in. I was frustrated about it for a long time. In my experience, it felt as if there were few rules and a lot of exceptions in language. Every time I thought I would have a good and grammatically correct sentence to say, a big fit of laughter emerged from my Norwegian friends. After so many years, they still tease me about the things I used to say or write incorrectly.

What I've noticed about a foreign language (I speak a couple of them) is that one learns it in layers. Moreover, with time, it gets deeper and deeper. It enters your subconscious until you eventually manage to master it bit by bit. Although my accent still betrays me, my understanding has become more complex.

For instance, at the beginning, you only speak the words and it is easy to trick yourself. Just because you speak the words, sometimes repeating them like a parrot, it does not mean you know what you are saying. The words you put together with the understanding and the syntax from your mother tongue do not lead to formulating the same meaning as the native speakers have.

Sometimes, a native speaker might guess that, most of the time, you don't mean what you are saying and help you through it. Otherwise, it might be a challenge to explain what you mean. Culturally, this might be a dangerous issue. In my experience, the native speaker expects that you understand much more than they are willing to explain. The reason for not being willing to explain is not because they do not want to; they don't know how to, perhaps because they never had to speak about it before. To locals, there isn't

easy way to explain their own culture
.... they grew up with and what has been
part of them for generations. It is the same in
every culture though. Just think for a minute...
If you are asked why people in your own culture
do things in the way they do, do you find it easy
to explain?

Many misunderstandings emerge from the
fact that we, the foreigners, speak the language
of the country we live in by translating word
for word our native tongue while expecting the
same result as in our culture of origin.

For instance, when I was a student, we had
a colleague from an Asian country. Every time
he made a new acquaintance, he would say, "It
gives me pleasure" instead of, "Nice to meet you."
At first, we laughed about it. Then, a woman
took him aside and explained that his way of
greeting people he met for the first time could
be misunderstood. He understood the point but,
on reflection, he was not saying anything wrong.
He just translated word for word the phrases he
used as a greeting in his native language.

It takes time to understand Norwegian
culture, and other cultures as well. I believe
that wherever one chooses to live, there are
social and cultural codes rooted in the language,

as well as specific ways of using words and making meaning. If we do not relate to them, it is because they never constituted an issue in our culture; therefore, there was no need for those words or expressions. Sometimes when I am with friends who speak the same languages as I do, we use words from the language we find that best describes a feeling or a situation.

Yet, I find that the more languages and cultures one manages to know, the richer one becomes.

The Art of Conversation

In my experience, Norwegian is not a very rich language, at least not anymore. Knut Hamsun's and Sigrid Undset's* days are long gone. Maybe this is the reason why the Norwegians are reputed for being very diplomatic.

Diplomacy comes naturally to many of them. One expression or word can be used in any situation and has meaning according to context. It is not a culture of "calling things by their name" even if North Norwegians are known by their keen for speaking from their "liver," which means very direct. My experience is that North Norwegians are direct in their speech when they are in the South. Being frank and direct might hurt people, and not hurting people with words is very important. This is why in meetings, for instance, one finds that discussions never end, while no one is willing to address the issue at hand.

Truthfully, there are many reasons for that.

One reason could be that they do not want to offend anyone; another would be that it is not their role to say something, as they do not have the suitable level of authority to address the matter. Respecting hierarchy and allowing the right words to come from the right people are important. Sometimes it might be better to avoid being the messenger since the messenger can be killed or ostracized, as the saying goes.

Another reason is that everybody, absolutely everybody participating in a meeting, needs to understand by themselves what goes on and what they need to do. A direct message, even if it comes from a boss, can be perceived as an order or a command. People are not used to this way of leading, except those working in the army. If someone feels that a work task is imposed, it will not be well-received. It is best if people take the initiative to do the task, as in this way they will be more productive. An important detail to mention here is that the intonation used when giving a work task, as well as the choice of words, are very important.

In other countries, languages can be used in direct or sharp ways, while words don't leave space for interpretation. It saves time. Moreover, sometimes people speak using vocal tones which are high or angry and irritated. Some Norwegians might perceive this as aggression, even if the speaker's intention is far from that. This is just the way they've learned speaking in their own cultures.

The words and the tone of voice are used with much care in North Norway as well, even if people here are regarded as "the Italians of the North" who are not afraid to speak up. Yet, in my experience, they speak up only in contexts where they know that what they say won't be used against them. Speaking like that to foreigners is safe for them, because these strangers will leave and won't hold what they've said against them. Many of them may not be that free in speech with other Norwegian peers. This might also be the reason why you won't find many Norwegians who ask you very personal questions when they meet you for the first time. When I say personal questions, I mean questions like, "Where do you work?" or, "How much do you earn?" or, "Are you married?" or, "Do you have children?" or, "Where do you live?" or, "How big is your family?" or, "Do you have siblings?" You may also find Norwegians will listen to the conversation you have with someone else before they say anything.

In this instance, for people coming from a culture with different views on individual privacy, it might seem that the Norwegians are not interested or don't care. It is not entirely true. Many of the Norwegians I've met were interested and curious, but it is not part of their culture to be direct from the start. They appreciate it when you tell your story first.

This aspect can be tricky though. If you disclose too much, it is not good either. Sometimes too much openness can be difficult, especially if you say too much about yourself and then expect people to share just as much when they are not willing to. As a result, following too much disclosure at the beginning, you may find that a person you thought you had a good connection with is now avoiding you.

People are very careful about what they share, so talking about the weather, food, restaurants, places to travel, hobbies, TV shows, or news is preferred. Everybody is comfortable with this kind of topic. Reading the local newspaper is important, and it can offer subjects of discussion that everybody can relate to.

From experience, asking many questions from the beginning signals a need for control, especially for us, from other cultures used to speed in mind and action. We want to see quickly where we are and how we can "control" the situation; and the more details we can find about our discussion partner, the easier it is to place them in a box in our mind. Placing people in "boxes" we created in our minds gives us a feeling of comfort and safety.

It is quite natural to feel the need for control when standing on foreign ground. The locals are at home. They know their situation and they know where they stand. We are only a new neighbor across the street or a new colleague at work. If they work together with us, then they will use that to find conversation subjects. However, they will not cross the line if they do not have to and, of course, if they are not drunk.

Spending a lot of time in their company is important. We do not have to talk to each other necessarily; it can be safe and comfortable to just be silent together. There is nothing wrong with silence as many people from more chatty cultures might think, mostly because they are not used to it and it can feel uncomfortable.

This experience became stronger once I traveled through my own country together with a Norwegian friend. Everywhere I went, I spoke with people I hadn't known before. Small sentences and short conversations in a relaxed tone at a shop or restaurant, in a park or in a taxi, etc. Strangers sitting next to us on the train or bus would tell me about their lives and struggles even if they knew they were not going to meet me again. I translated all the conversations to my Norwegian friend who was a bit confused and shocked about how personal the stories were. In my experience in Norway, few Norwegians share personal stories with a stranger on the bus or the train. In my friend's opinion, sharing your story with strangers was like "throwing pearls to the pigs." The belief is that your story and the details of your innermost life should not be given away at random. Confidants are carefully chosen and trusted for their discretion, as they won't give the story away to others but keep it safe as a precious stone. My friend also thought that the conversation was superficial and had no depth. This comment didn't make sense to me, because those people were telling us very personal stories—the kind that Norwegians don't share, not even after we have known them for decades. Later, I understood that my friend was measuring the theme of the conversations according to the time. If they were told fast, in a conversation with a stranger, then they were superficial because the amount of time used to get there was not the same as she was used to.

That was a perspective I hadn't heard before, and it made me understand how some Norwegian people perceive other people's lives and their roles in them. It also made it clearer to me the high value some may put on people and on the human needs.

* *Knut Hamsun's and Sigrid Undset are two of the most famous Norwegian classic writers. If you are learning Norwegian and you're at a good level, reading Norwegian classic literature can help you both with learning the language better and with increasing knowledge about how to understand the culture and its unwritten rules. After all, literature is, most of the time, based on reality. It is easier to call the truth literature than to tell it plainly in people's faces. It hurts less.*

Do It Yourself

"Did you knit that yourself?" one of my colleagues asked as she pointed at my woolen jacket.

"No," I answered and immediately saw a small expression of disappointment in her eyes.

Since I moved to North Norway, I have heard and I have been asked this question many times; and I've seen the disappointment on many people's faces following my negative answer. That goes for many things: baking, cooking, carpentry, painting, plumbing, electricity, and so on. It is as if people don't want to buy anything.

In student canteens and even in small cafeterias, the owner puts up notes that nicely ask people to help with cleaning by taking up the used plates and cups to the places especially designated for that. In other eating places, you order and pay at the counter then you get a small electrical device. When the device beeps, you pick up the food yourself from the kitchen area.

All this "lack" of service is noticeable in the price as well, compared to bigger restaurants where you have table service. The reasons are economical since the owner doesn't have to pay someone to do that job. There are still employees cleaning tables because the tourists are unaware of this rule if it is not written anywhere in English. It happens quite often in places where the probability of tourism from abroad is small. For foreigners coming to stay, it also takes a while to understand this.

A similar system exists at airports, where you can do the check-in yourself. Norway was one of the first countries to have self-check-in. I remember a British friend coming to visit in 2012 and being very frustrated by this, as she did not expect it. I didn't tell her either. After living here for so long, I simply forgot she was coming from a country that was more "service-oriented" at the time. Now, they have these machines in Heathrow as well.

It is the same system with your luggage if you come to Norway from another country. Even if your luggage is checked in to your destination, if you change flights in Oslo, you have to pick it up and check it in yourself, again, for your connecting flight within Norway.

In my experience, Norway is a "do it yourself" society.

When it comes to things around the house, cooking meals, baking, making jams, it is about having a nice atmosphere at home. There is a special word for it, "koselig," which means "enjoying, being comfortable, and taking your time to enjoy doing something alone or together with your friends and/or family." Having this special word enhances the "feeling" of an action. In English, there is the word "cozy," but it does not have quite the same meaning. Personally, I could not find a word which expresses the same thing in other languages.

If we talk about home improvement, painting, carpentry, fixing things, it also has to do with the fact that construction services are very expensive. The handier you are, the better it is for your bank account and your self-esteem. It feels so much better when you know that you can make things in your home and there is an emotional bond to them.

With time, I also understood that the "do it yourself" attitude has some social implications, too. It is easier to get in touch with people if you have a common interest. Of course, this is a general rule, but here it is a bit more important than in other places. For instance, if you belong to a knitting, sewing, hunting, fishing, or gardening club, you can socialize with people in that organized frame. It might be difficult to get to know them in other environments. It is possible that if you meet a person from your club in another social context, it could be difficult to improvise a conversation about other subjects except the club's theme, and it might even feel uncomfortable.

For those of us coming from societies where people are specialized in detailed work, and not used to doing many things by ourselves, this is new. It takes some time to understand that the society is built this way, and why things are like this. I think the welfare state has also been a contributing factor. When people live well, and have decent jobs and free time after work and on weekends, it is nice to have something else to do. Working with your hands is beneficial for both the mind and the soul. People are fed up with everything they find in shops, and they want to put their mark on things as an expression of well-being.

Homemade stuff is also often used for Christmas presents. Many grandmothers are making the traditional "lefse"* for their children. Other people are either frying almonds, baking gingerbread, or knitting woolen socks and mittens. In fact, these are the best Christmas presents. If you are good at making something, then that is what you should give people at Christmas or for other various occasions.

I guess Ikea has exploited this concept as well. After all, Ikea is Swedish.

__Lefse__ is a traditional soft Norwegian flatbread. It is made with potatoes (often, but not always), flour, butter, and milk or cream. Special tools are used to prepare __lefse__, including long wooden turning sticks and special rolling pins with deep grooves.

Gender Equality

Generally, Scandinavia is a territory where women are equal to men more often than in any other countries. Of course, there will always be a discussion about what "equality" means, but here, it is about tradition. Scandinavian countries never experienced slavery; the farmers have always been free, and the kings always had to rely on them. It would have been bad business not to listen to them or not to have their trust. The farmers had tenants, who were very poor people who would work the lands of the farmers for food, shelter, and very little money. They were never owned by their masters, yet even if they wanted, they wouldn't have been able to leave the estates they were working on because they were too poor. At the same time, it is important to mark that they were not slaves, bought and sold.

Moreover, the Norwegian Constitution abolished aristocracy in 1814.

Therefore, the idea that one person/human being, regardless of gender, would be owned by another has no roots here. Everyone is considered the same, and the idea of helping each other is familiar. Knut Hamsun's main character in "Growth of the Soil," Isak, needs "a woman's help," not a slave or a servant. He needs her "help," "kvinfolkshjelp" or "housekeeper," "husholdersker" as they say in Norwegian— expressed in one word, not two or three as in other languages, because the woman and the help that only she can provide are one.

Since the Viking times, men and women have fought wars, raised children, and taken care of the house/farm together. If men were not at war, they were fishing at sea. As they were gone for months during the fishing season, which is in winter, women had to deal with the children, the farm, and the stormy winters alone. Many would be widowed since the sea asked for its tribute. If women were good at leading a war or managing a farm, they would do that, while men helped with the household chores and the children, or vice versa. This is how the tradition was born—out of practical need.

Out of practical need, in 1839, women who were widowed or unmarried by the age of forty gained the right to work and earn money. In 1842, they gained the right to sell the products they had made. All this came from the fact that, at the time, there were more women than men in the country, and it would have been a burden to have them be supported by their fathers or brothers. It was better to let them work and earn their living.

By 1880, women ran more than 39% of the trade companies in Christiania (Oslo today). Therefore, in 1901, the next step for women who worked and paid taxes was to gain the right to vote; and by 1913, all women had the right to vote in Norway.

As a comparison, women gained the right to vote in New Zealand in 1893, next was Finland in 1906, and then Norway in 1913, followed by Iceland and Denmark in 1915, Russia in 1917, and Germany and Great Britain in 1918.

This succession of historical events leading to women's liberation is telling of how advanced the country is when it comes to gender equality.

Later, in 1969, Norway discovered oil, which meant a lot of money for education and research projects. In the '70s, gender equality researchers made it possible to analyze the roles of women and men in family and society. They found new definitions for what housework meant and how it should be distributed among adult family members.

This equality system can be difficult to understand by many foreigners coming from the South, where there are still many patriarchal social systems. One example is Switzerland where women did not have the right to vote until 1971 and, in the small region of Appenzzell Innerrhoden, women gained this right in 1991. Keep in mind that this is a European country. What about the rest of the world? You can do your research and find out when the women in your country gained this right. It may be interesting information.

The typical North Norwegian family has a mother, a father, and two children. Of course, each marriage has its own rules, all pretty much based on sharing both the house chores and the parental responsibility. Until I moved here (twenty years ago—things may have changed in the meantime), I had never seen so many men taking their babies on walks or to playgrounds as I did here. Both men and women can take paid maternity and paternity leave from work.

One may say, "Yes, but this benefit exists in many countries." Yes, but here, men, TAKE the time off. After speaking with many of them about this issue, I realized that bonding with their children can be just as important to them as it is to mothers. Many Norwegian men talk with pride about making dinner for their children, putting them to bed, or finding activities they can do together. Many families choose to take time off together so that both mum and dad are at home with the children. In this way, the children get a very good example of what a family should look like, and they bond with both their parents. After all, once they grow up, children do what they have seen happening in their families. Recently, there is an app making history. Samboer.app is designed to measure the housework each adult in the family is doing.

This freedom means that women and men can also break up faster. Another normal thing is not to get married at all, but just to live together as a family without necessarily having the papers. For some, this is a way of keeping each other on their toes, since they can break up anytime without much paperwork. And if they stay together without being married, it is proof of love. My Norwegian friends who've read this corrected me and said that, in many cases, if they have children, people do not need papers. They stay together for the sake of the children. Even more, if they reach the point of breaking up, they keep close and maintain a good relationship so children can grow up with both parents, even if they need to move houses every other week.

This makes many families with single parents; if the parents break up, the custody goes 50-50, and the children live with one parent every other week.

This is a very different attitude to many other societies where if people decide to break up, children become the woman's responsibility. Take a look at the culture you are coming from, and check some research, so you can put this into perspective.

Also, in terms of gender equality, Norwegian children grow up with different bedtime stories as well. For instance, *Pippi Longstocking* by the Swedish author Astrid Lindgren encourages them to build up a very different view about girls and women. Characters are strong, independent, smart—not sitting and waiting for the prince to rescue them, like *Snow White*, for instance. As teenagers, young girls can become much more like Anna from *Frozen* or *Mulan*.

Think for a moment, and remember which were your bedtime stories? Or were there any girls/women heroines of your childhood?

Living here for a good number of years, my understanding is that, for Norway, it's important that both men and women contribute to the household or to society. As the number of inhabitants is not very big in this country, it is difficult to imagine that half of the population, formed by women, wouldn't work. As a rule, women have their rights recognized and they are respected.

Even so, there is still a way to go to reach perfect equality. Perhaps, because it doesn't exist in our world, as we know it?

Phonic Pollution

One of the things I like in Norway is the way people speak to each other. I remember the first year here, when I could not understand the language. It was as if I was going through a cleaning process of my entire hearing system. My brain did not even take in a single swear word.

Until then, I didn't experience listening to my native language as an outsider. Even if it is a beautiful language, people speaking it can make it rather ugly. In many European cultures, and not only those, swear words and expressions are common even in the most "civilized" circles. Good friends can meet and say "hi" to each other with a swear word as well as a smile. Speaking ugly to each other can be a lot of fun, while in various friendship groups, coming up with as many and as nasty swear words as possible, can be an exciting competition.

Walking the streets anywhere in South Europe for instance, you could meet people swearing at you just because they do not like your face or your clothes, or the way you look. If you are a woman, you can be verbally harassed for both looking pretty or ugly. These comments come freely, and they are not asked for, especially from people you do not know and who do not know you either. They can also come from work colleagues. If you are "okay," you tolerate them because they are said with "love." If you are not "okay" and you protest, then you are a "bitch" who cannot take a "joke."

Years ago, during a Norwegian class, I remember we asked the teacher to teach us swear words. She took the task seriously and filled a blackboard with expressions and blushed while writing. I didn't understand why she blushed as none of those expressions contained references to intimate body parts, as is the case in many other cultures. The words were just variations of "hell" and "devil." People use synonyms so others wouldn't find the words offensive in conversation. Of course, these synonyms are well-known everywhere, and they are used mostly in Northern Norway where people are recognized for being more direct: "the Latinos" of the North.

I realized later that I could use Norwegian swear words with more ease than in my own language. Using those words meant nothing more to me than releasing frustration, but they said a lot to the Norwegians who happened to be around me. It pushed them away and made them avoid me for about a day. It took me a while to understand what was going on. It was much easier for me to swear in Norwegian as I didn't have an emotional connection with the language. It didn't "sit in my bones" at the time, like my mother tongue did. It's getting there though, after nearly twenty years of living in this country.

For some Norwegians though, since it is their mother tongue, the words mean much more. The words hit the core of their being, indicating that the person using them is just very angry right now and it is best to avoid them until he or she calms down. There is nothing so important that cannot wait, while the conversation can continue with everybody in the right mood.

Only then, once I understood that, I noticed I had the same behavior in reference to my own language as well. I didn't like people swearing or using "bad" words about each other; but at the time, I was so used to hearing it everywhere in my birth country, I hadn't thought about it in those terms. As a result, I became more careful with the words I would use myself, no matter the language I spoke. I started to appreciate even more the way in which most Norwegian people are cautious with their words. It is like being protected from unnecessary phonic pollution or from verbal harassment.

I am aware that there are also Norwegians who swear and especially in this part of the country that I live in. It depends on the environment and the amount of alcohol at hand. I know there are groups where creativity, when it comes to swear words, can be vivid. Yet, I was not "lucky" enough to visit them, and I cannot say I am sorry for it.

Differences in Teaching Methods

Bullying or harassment can be so ingrained in a culture that people find it hard to differentiate between them and a friendly and kinder teaching method. I believe it is essential to notice that bullying and harassment are not teaching methods, but forms of violence.

The Cambridge English Dictionary defines "harassment" as "behavior that annoys or upsets someone." I find that harassment and bullying exist in Norway too, but they often happen between friends and between people who know each other very well. As it happens, they might know how to or where to push someone's limits. Some bullies are good at saying that their behavior is "harassment." In this way, they give people they harass a chance to defend themselves. I rarely saw this coming from a teacher or from a leader. It doesn't mean it's not happening, but it's just less frequent; and I personally haven't experienced it often. I hear about and read about it in the newspapers.

In Norway, there is an issue with bullying among children and teenagers, but there are laws against it. Bullying is a form of violence, and it can have a devastating effect on people. Most parents are careful if something like this happens to their children. Eventually, they choose to move the children somewhere else if they don't feel right at school.

Unfortunately, in many other countries, making fun of students can be viewed as a teaching method and considered good pedagogy. If teachers and leaders use harsh tones or words, it can make children/pupils/students feel inadequate while experiencing people laughing at them. Some victims of bullying find it difficult to deal with the situation and end up closing themselves in and becoming introverts. Others play along by laughing back harder, attempting to hide their hurt. I simply could not help but notice this.

Perhaps, the purpose and the intention behind this method makes "people" out of children. Even teachers with a high level of consciousness use it without seeing that it does not fit with the principles of love, help, tolerance, and understanding.

I find it even more dangerous when people pay for a class or training, and the trainers use this method just to be funny. I see it as a lack of respect for those buying the class or training when they are paid to teach. It should be a good sign when people come to learn things from you. They don't come to be laughed at. This was one of the many reasons that contributed to my decision to leave my birth country. I simply did not understand why public humiliation was necessary in education when there are so many other ways of making people laugh and learn.

A few years ago, I took a specialized course in my field. I needed to learn some things in my language, so I could understand them better. Of course, one of the trainers decided it was funny to pick on seminar participants who were grown-up people. I spoke about it with some colleagues, but they didn't seem to understand they were subjected to bullying, as they did not know any better. They just kept laughing.

In psychology, there is the concept called "Stockholm syndrome," which describes a victim who falls in love with the aggressor and cannot live without this form of "love." People

I talked to didn't seem to understand that the abuse could deeply affect someone, even them. They said I was overreacting. Maybe. Although I still believe it is not the best way to teach or interact, especially when you meet people for the first time, and when they come to you for learning.

However, I do see a change unfolding. In the past five years or so, some of the new generations in my birth country, who did not experience either the war or the communist regime, are making a "psychological revolution."

Many read and educate themselves within the field and have started to talk about how war and dictatorship experiences (death, rape, hunger, anger, etc.) were passed down through generations and impacted them.

They are brave young people who dare take a deep dive into themselves and their family histories and try to heal whatever they can, so they won't continue to pass the wounds to their children.

I hear them speaking about these issues, and I also see a rising interest in mental and emotional health. Much more than in Norway at the moment, I must say.

The Child King

The concept of children as "Kings" and "Queens" is a special one. We do not often come across it, even if it makes sense. Children are our future. The way we take care of them shows how we take care of our future. Therefore, the way we raise our children is important. Norway and Scandinavia are generally very aware of this and are known to be countries where children are raised in particular ways.

We, who grew up in former communist countries, need to keep in mind that our cultures were deliberately held back in many areas of study such as psychology and parenting, for instance. Following the Second World War, Western Europe and Scandinavia rebuilt their societies in freedom while Russia and Eastern Europe experienced communism as a social experiment.

When I arrived in Norway for study, I quickly noticed the difference in mentality and way of thinking between students from the former Communist Bloc, North America, Latin America, Africa, and those coming from Western Europe and the Nordic countries. At the time, it felt to me that many of the Western and Nordic students seemed way too sensitive. I couldn't quite grasp what it was.

Later, once I made Norwegian friends, I asked them questions that helped me understand why everything was so different from what I'd known before. With time, I realized that it was linked to the way they were brought up. My friends explained that Norwegian Law and the child protection system are well-developed. When they are ten years old, children learn about their rights at school. They also know that the law protects them if something wrong happens at home. Children are told about sexual abuse, physical violence, addiction, alcohol consumption, and many other issues.

Moreover, teachers and educational staff are obliged by law to inform the authorities if they believe that something of concern might happen in a child's family. At that point, the Child Protection gets involved with the family and sometimes this might lead to the children being removed from their parents. Child protection is an aspect which is taken very seriously in Norway.

In my communist childhood, I witnessed violence, both at school and in people's homes. The socio-political system often used violence to keep people under control; being silent meant "being good" and staying safe, for fear of the system. Although Nordic countries have their ways of keeping people silent, direct and blunt violence is not something people are silent about.

Here, the "fear" revolves around other people's opinion about you or about being left out of social groups. In a country with a few million people, social isolation is an important issue, unlike in other countries with tens of millions of people who live and work in the same space. Another Nordic way to maintain silence is by giving everybody a roof over their head and a full stomach. If everybody has their primary needs met, and no one is visibly starving, the need to protest is not that urgent.

As I was beginning to understand why the culture here was so different in this aspect, (child upbringing, and sensitivity), I came across one of the most prominent child psychologists in the world and some of the books she wrote. As I read some of her books and her personal story, all the pieces of the puzzle fell into place for me. Her name is Alice Miller, and she is the first psychologist to write about what it is like to be a child and about the various feelings a child experiences. You can search her name and all her work will come up.

I remember growing up with the notion that "children should be seen, but not heard," and with regular violence and bullying at school and at home. They were considered "teaching methods." It felt as if children were not human beings, but just "something" with no feelings, "something" born only because the system required it. During the Cold War, abortions were illegal in Romania, while mothers who had given birth to at least four children were acknowledged as "hero mothers." It was the way women contributed to growing the country's labor force. This was a different kind of "baby boom" from the rest of Europe, ordered by the communist state in 1966. In their book, *Freakonomics*, Steven Levitt and Stephen J. Dubner speak about how this kind of decision has impacted the lives of the children born this way.

Norway was not much different either. If you talk to people born before 1960, some even younger, and they open about their lives, you can hear many stories of child abuse, domestic abuse, oppression, and colonization of indigenous people. These things are part of history, and we cannot deny nor avoid them.

However, the difference here is that, during the '70s, people in the medical system came across Alice Miller's books and took them seriously. The newfound knowledge and understanding were implemented and embedded into the social system. Many people I know remember Trond Vigo Torgersen who showed up on national TV one evening in 1972 and declared that from that day forward, it was forbidden to hit children in Norway. It resulted in a child protection system that puts children first. This can confuse many immigrants for whom children's rights are a foreign notion.

For those curious to find and read Alice Miller's books, you will find research she did on people who shaped history. Hitler and Ceausescu among them, she explains how their childhood trauma had influenced their behavior as adults. If you understand Norwegian, you can search for a TV show produced by the Norwegian National Television (NRK) about Alice Miller. Her experience as a survivor during WWII motivated her to study psychology and to specialize in child psychology.

Who's "Discriminating" Whom?

I have been living in this country for a while now. As a result, I get invited to parties where I happen to be the only foreigner. A couple of years ago, one of my friends had a birthday party and, again, I was the only foreigner in a gathering of ten Norwegians.

Among other subjects, the topic of being "not from town" came up. Three people were from the town I lived in, and the rest, up to ten, from other smaller towns all over Norway. They complained about how difficult it was for adults to make friends in a foreign town. If you move to Norway alone, for work, or even with a spouse, it is difficult to know people that you can call friends. It takes more than a couple of random meetings and casual talks until, eventually, after a year or more, people would accept a new person. The issue of integration in a new place doesn't apply only to foreigners, but to Norwegians as well, even if they are in their own country. So, it is not a surprise that we, as foreigners, encounter the same problem.

Following that conversation, someone talked about foreigners "discriminating" against the Norwegians. The context was parties organized by immigrants, to which they didn't invite Norwegians. One lady remarked, "They seem to have a wonderful time among themselves, gossiping about Norwegians and the things we do, so we feel left out."

It made me think about a similar comment I had heard when I was still a student many years ago. I was involved with an organization dealing with foreign students' welfare. I remember organizing lots of trips and parties and events, not only for international students, but for Norwegian students, too. We would send emails and put up posters around the campus and the student flats with information about what, where, and when, costs, and so on. Very rarely would Norwegian students show up. I remember how a classmate told me that the Norwegians would feel left out from the "wonderful time you guys have."

I didn't understand what she meant, and I put up more posters around our building. I also invited her personally to one party, explaining that they just needed to come as they were welcome. Still, not much luck. The woman didn't show up and only a few Norwegian colleagues came. I didn't realize then that the Norwegians needed more time to feel comfortable and safe in a "foreign" environment. When I say "foreign," I don't mean another country or people from other nationalities, but simply people they did not know. It didn't matter if they were from other countries or the same nationality as them. A good amount of the Norwegian people I know, still today, find it difficult to speak with other Norwegians they don't know. It is a cultural thing.

Thinking about it now, with the information gathered about Norwegian culture in the last two decades, I would do it differently. I would speak with each Norwegian classmate, approach him or her personally, and even offer to pick them up and bring them to the place. I would then not leave their side and stay with them all night long, so they feel secure and comfortable while they "know someone" at that party and don't have to deal with strangers all by themselves. Eventually, I'd introduce them to everyone at the party and choose familiar conversation subjects, so they feel safe with at least one topic of discussion. I found out later that this is called having "social skills" in the Norwegian context.

I didn't know that then. In the world I came from, "social skills" meant being able to speak with everybody, with all sorts of people. It didn't matter if I knew them from before or not. I was an international student, feeling "okay" speaking English, joking, and talking freely with strangers. I didn't understand why it was so complicated for them, even if the information about Norwegians being "shy" had been shared with us. "Shy" was a very foreign concept to us. We were already speaking at least one foreign language, and we had already traveled abroad at least once. At the time, it seemed that few Norwegian students did and they didn't talk much about interacting with locals, whatever country they had been to. Mostly, I have heard stories about cheap food and drinks and shrimp cocktails.

They were simply intimidated by our self-confidence and freedom of action. In those times, many Norwegian students weren't so comfortable speaking English either. They were afraid of making mistakes and, consequently, shamed themselves when they did. Making a fool of themselves was terrifying. We, the international students, made many errors when speaking English as well; but we didn't care. I feel the need to mention that this story is almost twenty years old. The children born then have learned English by now. Today, it might feel like "all Norwegians" speak English. Still, I would dare to disagree. There are parts of the country where people don't; or if they do, they don't like it.

So, the Norwegian students preferred not to come to our party. Plus, at the party, we did some "outrageous" dancing as soon as we got there. I remember going out on Saturdays at 10:00 pm and starting to dance right away. My friend and I were the only ones on the dance floor, and Norwegians would look at us with pity, probably thinking that we were already drunk. Neither I nor my friend were drinking. We just liked to dance, and we didn't need alcohol to do so.

I guess that by telling this story, I can explain a bit the reasons why both categories, immigrants and Norwegians, feel discriminated against. There is a big difference in the party style and in the amount of time each group needs to start a conversation. Again, it is about "time," as I explained in an earlier chapter. To immigrants, *time passes* and to Norwegians, *time comes*.

If you understand the concept of time coming, slowly, and find a way to make it work for you, everything is fine. With time, and some investment from your part, the community of Norwegians will embrace you.

Cheers—or Alcohol and Politics

I guess everybody who has met Norwegians has also seen the twinkle in their eyes when the subject of "alcohol" is brought up. Or maybe, you've encountered big smiles when they see a bottle of wine. The Norwegians say it is a smile "all around the head, if the ears would not be in the way."

There is a drinking culture everywhere. Yet, in Norway, this is different. In my experience, in the rest of Europe, people might drink a glass of wine every evening at dinner. It is nice, as it enhances the taste of the food. It's cozy. No need to get drunk, just enjoy it and still be able to work the next day. Yet, in Norway, people drink "all the glasses" or more on Friday and Saturday evenings, and then nothing for the rest of the week. In the last few years, in addition to the weekend drinking, some have also adopted the

European way of drinking during weekdays as well. You can do the math.

The reason it became like this is because the state has a monopoly on alcohol. If it is over 4.5% you can only buy in special stores called "Vinmonopol." Drinks with up to 4.5% alcohol, one can buy in grocery stores but only until 18:00 hours.

In pubs and restaurants, it is really expensive. One beer can be up to 10 euros and a glass of wine up to 25 euros.

Making beer or fruit wine can also be a hobby for some people. As long as it is for personal use, it is allowed. It's forbidden to sell it. This hobby can go so far that people are making their own personal brands and labels. It can be quite fun.

Some years back when I first moved into my current home, I was much more into drinking alcohol than I am now. (I guess it's age. I get terrible headaches the next day, and I don't think it's worth it.) It was a Monday evening, and I sat on the stairs having a cigarette and a glass of whiskey. My neighbor came out of her house, saw me and asked surprised, "What are you doing?"

I responded, "I'm relaxing! Cheers!" I raised my glass, "Do you want some?"

She looked at me terrified and responded, "It's Monday!"

From her body language, intonation, and the way she looked at me, I understood I was doing something outrageous. She did try my fine whiskey though, by the way, with the guilt and the excitement of doing something forbidden. Since alcohol was and still is a state monopoly in Norway, it is the "forbidden fruit," and especially on a Monday.

Still, on Friday afternoons, my work colleagues look so happy when going to buy wine, just like kids happy to get candy. Getting drunk on the weekend is a popular sport, for both men and women. A glass together or a hard party only brings couples closer. If they have children, both mum and dad take turns to look after them on weekends, so that the partner can go out and party (drink) with friends. The fact that both partners need a break from family life stands high in this culture.

No one speaks badly of drunk people, except if it is a serious issue when the social system gets involved. It is perfectly "okay" to be drunk and perfectly "okay" to have a hangover. This is different from my birth country where people are severely judged if they can't hold their drink.

There, it is "okay" to drink but not "okay" to be so drunk that you lose it. Of course, people in my country of origin are not the most tolerant people in the world. It's cultural.

In Norway, it is not permitted to drink during work hours. Yet, to keep employees' morale high, many workplaces organize wine lotteries. There are hundreds, if not thousands, of rules about the Friday wine lottery. It is mostly used to gather people together for a common interest. Even if they don't like each other, they all love wine. It is easy to be cut off from social groups if you're not drinking, so everybody must drink alcohol at parties. Otherwise, those who drink would feel embarrassed if one person is not. That is because some would get so drunk that they'd forget what they said or did. The thought that one person was sober all along and will remember everything the following day is a terrifying prospect.

That is why people don't take pictures at parties either. What happens there stays there, and it is not documented in any way. However, the young generation does not always follow this rule. Young people take pictures of their drunk friends and spread them over the internet. It is called harassment and the officials try to stop it. If they manage, that is another question.

I remember a lady telling me once how happy she felt that her youngest son was going out drinking. In this way, he chose to socialize, and being out drinking was much better than being alone and depressed in his flat. Something else the lady said was that getting so drunk that you wouldn't know yourself is a sign of strength. It meant that you were sure of yourself and transparent, that whatever would come out while being unconsciously drunk would not be a threat to you when sober.

Again, reading the newspapers around Christmas time, with stories about drunk sex that breaks families up, or puts work colleagues in difficulty, we see it is still an issue.

In recent years, I've also come across silent movements against alcohol. Usually those who decide to protest drinking are children brought up in homes where alcohol was an issue. There are even some organizations fighting for children who are growing up in these kinds of homes, and you can check some of those websites here:

www.bar.no, www.voksenforbarn.no
www.dinutvei.no, www.plikt.no
www.snakkemedbarn.no, www.jegvilvite.no

Age CAN Be Just a Number

On this topic, what I like about North Norway is people's attitude about their age. Age is spiritual, and not referred to by the actual number of years.

When I spoke about going to visit my family in my birth country, I was asked how old my mother was. As my mother aged, my answer varied too, from fifty-four to past seventy today. When my mum was between fifty-four and about sixty-seven, the comment I heard most was, "She is very young." My experience so far is that in Norway, people are allowed to be as young as they want. Life can be joyful. At least this is what they say upfront. The complaints are only for select ears.

People can afford to be "children" much longer than we're used to in Southern Europe or other corners of the world. I discovered a similar attitude in my French, Italian, Spanish, or

Southeast European friends. If you are forty, you need to retire or go home and wait to die, as life is over for you. A forty-year-old Syrian refugee, for example, is considered by his or her society very old. I was helping with an integration course led by the municipality some time ago, and I saw the reaction of the group of refugees when they heard that my colleagues' ages were fifty-nine and sixty-four. Their estimation went as far as forty-five and fifty-five.

Another time, a colleague was very happy when she was about to reach her fortieth birthday, as she got "old". She comes from an African country and, in her culture, at this age you've passed your youth and become old. If you are old, everybody respects you and asks for your opinion. You also gain status in your community. I didn't tell her that the number of years one lives is not always relative to the wisdom acquired. We can find many old people behaving childishly. After all, we are all children inside. It is just that in some cultures, the harsh life does not allow the children to be children. They become adults before their time. And in other cultures, welfare allows people to be children for a very long time, since they are not required to take responsibility. Norway is such a welfare country that I have seen in practice how, until forty, life is research in development. You start living at forty, a belief that is in opposition to what I was led to believe in my country of origin where life conditions during my upbringing were much more difficult.

People I came across here, and who allowed me to take a peek into their lives, get married late if they do at all; and they live life to the fullest for as long as they can. If they marry early and find out on the way that they've grown apart, they separate and build a life with somebody else or on their own, while doing the things they love and enjoying time with their children if they have them. After all, children are much better off with two happy separated parents than with two miserable parents living together.

A general rule I discovered here is that children are "mine, yours and ours." I have a friend who remarried at forty with a fifty-year-old guy who had also been married before. They have one child, as a testimony of their love for each other, and the fifty-year-old guy was the one to stay at home with the baby. They both have three children each from previous marriages, and the youngest was the joy of the whole family. They travel together as a family, walk up the mountains, work, and have a good time. Of course, this was the outside picture, visible to me; but the point is, that they are not "old" at fifty or sixty, as they might be considered in other countries.

The welfare state contributes to this as well. For instance, when I heard people saying that my mother was young at sixty-five, I felt the need to explain that sixty-five in Southeast Europe is not the same as sixty-five in Norway. Norway did not experience, let's say, in the past 150 years (for the sake of a brief dive into older history of Southeast Europe), one independency war, two world wars, and fifty years of communism. Norway had only the second World war that was a shared common bad experience and, of course, poverty until 1969 when oil was discovered. Scandinavia was somehow more stable in that sense than the rest of the world; therefore it had time for the society to develop slowly and peacefully.

My mother worked night shifts at a factory while having four children and a husband who was working two jobs. On top of that, there was no food in stores during communism and it was a struggle to find it. People had to be best friends or bribe those who worked at a grocery store if they wanted bread on the table. Food was not a problem for those part of the communist elite. I guess that all the stress accumulated then, adds more weight to the concept of "age." So no, sixty-five in southeast Europe is not the same as sixty-five in Norway.

In North Norway, among the couples I know, some do not have children yet. Therefore, each partner spends Christmas or parts of the summer holiday at his/her parents' house and takes time to be a child for a while longer. Only when children come into the picture do couples consider it is the end of their childhood.

If couples get help with the children from their parents, they consider themselves very lucky, and they express it. They do not take this help for granted. In one seminar, I heard a sixty-year-old Southeast European woman talking about her "grandma duties." In many families from Southeast Europe, the expectation is that grandparents get involved in their grandchildren's lives; and they are given responsibility in their upbringing. They are not paid for that and often this help can be just taken for granted. This does not always happen in Norway. Some grandparents consider themselves lucky to be part of their grandkids' lives, but they can choose the time they want to spend with them. If they want to travel and not be involved in their grown-up children and grandchildren's lives, then they don't do it. They travel, see the world, and don't care that much if someone would call them "selfish" for not "helping out."

Another detail I think might contribute to Norwegians' youthfulness is the language. They have no polite pronouns. Respect is shown through attitude, not words. People are called by their first names, regardless of their age or social status. Ordinary people can approach even the Prime Minister with "Hei Jens" (Stoltenberg), or "Hei Erna" (Solberg) and now "Hei Jonas" (Gahr Støre) and they will be answered back politely and with a smile. People forget their age if they are not constantly reminded that they are a "Madam" or "Sir."

By contrast, as soon as I step off the airplane in my country of birth, someone swiftly shows me their respect by calling me "madam" or "lady." But I do not always feel their respect in their attitude or in their voice. It is just a word. Sometimes it feels nice, then I wake up suddenly to the reality that the age on my ID card is a different number that I feel in my heart.

I recognize this in the words and the attitudes of my friends, the same age as me, but still living there. It feels like they are slowly marching to the cemetery. I don't think they are aware of it, and if I pointed that out to them, they look at me with confusion, saying, "Stop being so Norwegian." As if me becoming Norwegian is their main concern.

Anyway, my point is that age can be looked at as just a number and we are all children. In Norway, if a sixty-year-old person becomes widowed or divorced, it is perfectly normal to find someone else to share the rest of their days with, without being judged by society. It is a natural thing to do. The children are also happy when their parents are not alone and can still enjoy life in someone's company. The retiring age is between sixty-two and seventy; and if the health allows, people are strong and green many years after that. It helps that they keep physically active, walking up mountains and running marathons, skiing, kayaking, and doing all sorts of other sports.

In Norway I have learned that people are as old as they want to be, and they get help with that.

To Know vs. Knowing

In North Norway, the time and the age of a relationship, how long it takes two people to get to know each other is very important, much more important than the experience shared.

I find there is a dilemma here. The meaning of "to know" in different cultures. I think there are more meanings to this verb, which expresses an abstract "action." One meaning is about knowing a subject, knowing how to do a job or how to be a specialist in something, or knowing a person. As many of us experience, there is always room to improve in a subject. There are always new theories that come out and there is always a time when you need to learn even more about the field you thought you knew all about.

I find it is interesting to observe how the verb "to know" is used when it concerns other people. We are beings who learn something every single day, and sometimes it is difficult to say that we know someone very well. We have no idea what kind of brain cell connections or emotional processes take place in ourselves every single second. How can we say about another person that we know him or her? We all experience that even when we've "known" someone for many years, we still discover new things about a person, actions or behaviors that we never expected.

Living abroad, I find that there is a need to experience various behaviors when it comes to knowing someone. As ex-pats/immigrants, no matter where we come from, we all have in common the fact that we live in a country other than our own. We feel a bond and a connection with other fellow ex-pats because we live similar experiences.

Another bond emerges between people with the same country of origin and living in the same adoptive country. Here there is also the same language that brings people together, the same food, the same traditions. At the same time though, one must consider that maybe some migrated abroad because of the people, the traditions, the food. They do not necessarily need to meet up with people from the same country of origin as them, as maybe they had enough of them already, in their own country. As harsh as this might sound, it is true in many cases.

In these groups, I find that sometimes people forget that not everybody wants to be friends with everybody. Even back in their own country, people weren't friends with everybody, as this is simply impossible. One can be polite with strangers, but this is another story. So, just because two people speak the same language, and they are nice and polite, it does not necessarily mean that they can automatically be BFFs (Best Friends Forever).

In North Norway, I discovered that people can be more careful about how they use the phrase "to know somebody." It lies in the use of the language, and therefore in the culture.

a. About a person they have known for many years, since school, for instance, they will say exactly this, "We went to the same school together, and we've been classmates." Short and explicit. They do not say "I know that person," as they didn't know him or her in all aspects of their life, nor after they finished school. If you deal with a talkative person, you might also get, " I used to know that person a little, at that time. I can't say I know him or her now," and probably they will follow up with a story from those times.

b. About someone they have heard about, they will say, "I know who he or she is, but I do not know him or her personally." Again, very simple, explicit, and honest.

c. To a person they've met for a short while, during a short meeting or a course, or a trip, they will say at the end, "I am glad that I've got the chance to get to know you a little." This means, "I cannot say I know you very well. After all, it would have been impossible to get to know you in all aspects of your life in only a couple of days. But it was nice to meet you and share this experience for these past few days." Again, polite and objective.

During my first years in Norway, I could not understand why, when traveling on work trips or seminars, people from the same firm or the same department would stay together and not mix, nor express an interest in getting to know people from other firms or departments. Now, after many years, I understand that all they wanted to do on those trips was just get to know each other even better. This is something I do not often experience between ex-pats or immigrants.

They are happy to get acquainted with other people as well, and they are open to talk to even more people. I have also experienced that traveling with my work colleagues and expressing an interest in meeting new people has always brought a shadow of sadness to their faces. At first, it took me a long time to understand that my words were received and interpreted as a "rejection" of the group on my part. And it was not what I intended at all. For me, the trips were about "networking" while I found out that meeting new people can be experienced by some Norwegians as tiring and as an action that demands a lot of work—work, which many people who are content and established in their own country, family, group of friends, simply do not want to do.

I noticed the same "sadness" in my Norwegian friends' body language when, being invited to dinner, I used to leave soon after the meal was finished. It had never crossed my mind that it could have been interpreted as an offense. I did not know then that the whole point about the dinner invitation was the "after dinner time" when people sit in the living room, drink coffee or a stronger digestive, and chat about all and nothing. That was the time for bonding, for creating an experience by talking about the meal and food recipes, and slowly, the discussion would become more interesting with real-life stories, which allowed the group to build a stronger bond. This "bonding" could take many hours of the night—nights, which I am rarely comfortable with not sleeping through.

Writing this paragraph, I feel like I am stating the obvious; and yet what is obvious to me, might not be obvious to someone else, and the other way around.

Coming back to "knowing" people, I have noticed in some ex-pats or immigrants (in my experience, many from "Latin" corners of the world) a very familiar behavior as well as a way of speaking which one could see as being careless. Maybe they've met a person once, but the speech is very sure and confident, "I KNOW him or her. I met them a couple of days ago." It can be misleading. I may have worked with people in the same corridor for years, but I cannot say "I know them." I am acquainted with some small aspect of their lives as we interact through work tasks. Some work leaders may have invited us to their homes for a department dinner or Christmas party; but still, I cannot say, "I know them." Otherwise, I am on completely foreign ground, in each new situation which brings us together, even if there is a familiarity brought by seeing each other every day, and through the gossip which inevitably happens in each workplace.

So, I still consider the question: What does it mean to KNOW somebody? Do you know yourself?

Perfumes and North Norway

Did you ever meet a person who'd left behind a trace of perfume? How was it?

In my experience, that feeling can be nice when the amount and the quality of perfume are just right, and it only enhances the impression one can make over the person wearing it. I assume it is common knowledge that perfumes can have unique fragrances in accordance with the unique person who chose it.

On top of that, there are some more factors which influence how a perfume complements a person's presence, or it makes a less agreeable impression. Consider the following:

- Is the perfume applied directly on the skin, or is it sprayed?

- Is it the perfume sprayed in the air, and then the person passes through the perfumed air?

- Is the perfume sprayed on clothes?

- Does the perfume come from the shower gel or from the body lotion?

- Is the perfume applied on a washed body or on a body who just woke up, instead of washing?

- Is the perfume used in large quantities or is it used discreetly?

- How is the humidity of the air we are walking through every day, outside or inside?

This last aspect, I think, is overlooked by many people who move to North Norway. The humidity of the air is very important if one is to wear perfume.

While living here, I noticed I cannot use the same perfumes I once used in South Norway or even further South of Europe. I realized that I need both different labels as well as different amounts.

In North Norway (Scandinavia, Canada, Russia), I am using very little perfume—less than one puff, or no perfume at all. The shower gel is more than enough, and even this can sometimes be too much. Otherwise, it spreads all over my office and the rooms I walk through every day, and it can take a while for it to disappear.

In South Norway and Europe, I can use a bit more, up to two puffs. No danger if I use more. It won't hurt that much. I was surprised by the difference, until I realized it had to do with the humidity of the air.

Warm air in South of Europe holds more water, which means that perfume vapors spread through the air and mix with a bigger quantity of vaporized water. It makes the fragrance less aggressive, but pleasant and fresh.

Cold air in the North of Europe holds much less water, which means the intensity of the perfumes will be much stronger and the effect will be the opposite of agreeable if used in the same quantity by someone in warm countries.

Crossing buildings made of wood, I noticed many times that strong scents which I recognize from the South of Europe. It convinced me that someone from a warm country had just passed through. Sometimes we need to open windows and doors as the smell is too much to bear. If anyone around is allergic, or has asthma, then it is even less fun.

Often there are signs in workout centers, hospitals and medical centers, schools and especially kindergartens that raise the attention of not wearing perfumes at all, because people may be allergic to them.

I am sure the intention of the person wearing the perfume is good, but because of the humidity in the country we live in, it is important to consider when one leaves home.

I guess the reason I chose to write about such a small, everyday detail, is that I noticed how mostly foreigners use more perfume than necessary, maybe because it is something they used to do in their country of origin. No harm meant, yet the effect can be damaging. I have heard enough comments, which could be avoided. Believe it or not, such a small detail can contribute to accepting or rejecting a foreigner.

It is the same with the temperature. Five degrees below zero in a dry atmosphere in the far North will feel like plus five in very humid air, further South, in a temperate climate. This is why as far North as I live, it is not as cold as people from the South may think.

Winter Driving with Spike Tires

There is a season for driving challenges on our Nordic roads.

I drive a lot in my commute to town. In winter time, the weather is moody and ice is everywhere; and the roads are blocked because of some big trucks that are not equipped with winter tires, and they glide on the slippery roads. Even if locals equip their cars with spike tires and chains during these times, it does not seem that the information gets to the foreign drivers who come from the south.

I realize it is difficult to understand that snow and ice can be cold, slippery, and wet, especially when you see it on TV or only in pictures. A friend from the southern part of the world helped explain this when she showed up at my door wearing fluffy textile short boots and no socks, without warm and proper clothing. She'd rented a car from town which was equipped, but the path from the parking lot to my house was up to her knees with snow. The water went straight through her thin clothes and shoes. She was shocked and upset as her expensive trendy boots were ruined and she needed to spend more money to buy clothes suitable for the Norwegian winter. She needed wool clothing close to the skin and a warm waterproof jacket, trousers, and boots. And that was no joke.

It is a similar issue with the big transport companies from the south, which do not understand that in Scandinavia, and even more so in North Scandinavia, the winter is harsh and long (sometimes up to six months); and you need to spend extra money in order to keep safe on the roads.

A simple google search can show the rate of the accidents in the area. The police have the habit of taking all the big trucks off the road to check them for proper equipment. Therefore, if you are a truck driver heading North during the winter (October – May), then you should ask your employer to help you equip your truck. Otherwise, don't drive!

Onion Style and Rubber Boots

M ost of us migrate from the South. We notice quite quickly a different dress code in the North. There is a saying here: "There is no such thing as bad weather, only bad clothing."

I entirely agree with it. When you live in a country where the weather changes from sunshine to rain to snow and then to sunshine again in only a few hours, it isn't easy to choose clothing. Almost everybody wears a kind of rain/wind/snow jacket on top of their clothes. The "layered" way of dressing is the most practical. I call it "onion style." It means that you dress with layers of clothes, which you can take or put on according to what happens during the day or night.

The shoes are also special. Rubber boots in cute colors and design matched with woolen socks can be the most elegant thing you have ever seen. Also, boots are convenient when there are tons of melting snow or when it pours down rain and there isn't a dry place where you can walk on the streets. Sportswear is also in fashion everywhere and at all times.

Here, up North, people are most passionate about nature and outdoor activities. The type of outdoor activity equipment can tell you about a person's status: the type of bike, kayak, parachute, skies, boat, and so on. Only after that comes the house, the car, the iPhone, unlike many other European countries.

In my attempt at becoming entrepreneurial, I have attended quite a few seminars and business presentations and courses, so I could see what it takes. In some of these business presentations, it was refreshing to see the way very successful people dressed—casual and with woolen socks coming out from the short leather, well-worn short boots. That did not stop them from giving a brilliant presentation and showing us how they came to their success.

On one rainy day, a woman showed up with a beautiful, colorful rain jacket and rubber boots up to her knee. Woolen socks were visible under those. Elegant and chic in a daring way, a look that I rarely see in the South of Europe in the business world.

People only wear suits or fancy dress at Christmas parties, weddings, and around age numbers (40, 50, 60...) birthday parties and at baptisms. Sometimes when they go out on the weekends. When I first moved here, I wore jeans and trainers for a whole year. I was fed up with the dress code and the tiresome high heels I had to wear in my previous jobs before I moved to Norway. Everybody wears sneakers with everything: dresses, suits, even with evening gowns. When people like to walk, and there are long distances between places, there is no point in wearing fancy shoes. The roads, even in Oslo, are not built for that. Recently, I see this fashion traveling south, which is a good sign for the backs of the ladies who may choose it instead of high heels.

I like that very few people up here care about this aspect. If you walk through various institutional buildings, you can see people with shorts and sandals. Sometimes socks and sandals are also in fashion, or no shoes at all. Of course, there are exceptions, especially in the capital, and in the finance industry mainly; and there are not many immigrants working there. At the same time, Norway is much bigger than its capital.

When you spend all day in front of a computer, it is essential to feel comfortable. Furthermore, in all flights I've taken from Oslo up here, I've encountered the "no shoes policy." At the beginning, I thought it was weird and impolite, but after a few years I started to do the same. If you wonder, it does not smell. People tend to wash, and this is more important than a dress code.

There is also a custom that says that one has to take his or her shoes off when visiting someone's house. It is about being polite and having respect for the host who cleans the house. It wouldn't be nice to get inside a nice home after walking through rain, snow, wind, and mud. Norway is a "do it yourself" country and having house help is not as common as in other countries. However, this habit is not specific only to the Northern cultures. We find it in other countries as well.

To conclude, North Norwegians dress for comfort, which is a significant value in society. Nobody understands why women would want to break their backs by wearing high heels. Does it make them more beautiful? Not in Norway. The beauty of many Norwegian women comes from inside. It is something one feels, and learns to see. I also rarely hear about women being "beautiful" (vakker/pen), which is the outside beauty. Most often, I hear about women being "great" (flott), which expresses something that could be translated as "beautiful inside-out."

The Invisible Luggage

People move a lot, generally. Move from one house to another, from one city to another, from one country to another. But why? What is it that makes them choose "the moving" move?

In my experience, people move because they believe that they will feel better somewhere else. They will have a better job, better friends, better living standards, better experiences, and so on. For many though, moving does not necessarily mean a change for the better. When you move, you don't just take with you the visible luggage such as suitcases or parcels sent by post, you also take invisible luggage such as culture, values, and past experiences.

Some experiences are good to have whilst others are best left behind. Sometimes we need to just put them aside until the right time comes to be taken out again, as we need to heal and say goodbye to them for good. Otherwise, they will weigh us down. How do we manage to do that? To leave behind experiences, habits, ways of being? It is like being asked to leave behind a foot or a hand.

When a visible wound appears, one needs time and patience for healing. People go to the doctor and take painkillers in order to take away the symptoms. But when it comes to feelings, ideas, culture, experiences, behaviors, which are "invisible," things get complicated. Even with the right support from people around us, sometimes we are unable to accept the support. We can be the toughest judges of ourselves. We can be stuck and so full of invisible old patterns that we do not manage to take in new ones. Just like a cup. To be filled up, it must be emptied out first. If we are already "full," how can we take in new knowledge and experiences? What if the things that fill us are invisible? Because they are invisible, we do not know how to ask for help and eventually go to see a therapist who can help us empty the cup. If "therapy" is taboo both in the societies in which we have been born and raised and the new society we have chosen to live in, then there are even smaller chances to be able to "empty" the cup.

Observing people around me, the invisible stuff can be just as painful as a physical wound. Instead of letting that pain out, people prefer to hide it deeply into their hearts and cover it with different distractions: wine, food, cigarettes, laughter, smiles, drugs, shopping, traveling, and other things which make us feel good momentarily. The illusion of feeling good and coping makes us believe that everything is fine, and we never speak of them.

If they are spoken about, they can become ways in which we accuse others. It is the other's fault. It is easier to point the finger at others than face our own invisible wound.

This invisible luggage tends to create the new reality in the new country; and somehow, it shapes the new environment. Some may feel that the only thing they changed is their geographical place on the map, or the language, or the system of rules to follow in the working world. Otherwise, the experiences they run from stay the same. The histories repeat themselves, even thousands of miles away from the country of origin—in another language and with other people. It's like a theater production, played by different actors, in a different language, yet the subject is the same.

To avoid this, some groups stick together. Usually these are people who did not learn nor can they speak the language of the new country that well. It is easier that way. To gather and be together, to create a similar environment with the one experienced in the country of origin, makes the adjustment to a new country much easier. Here, in safety, old values keep on living longer. People do not entirely disregard the values in their new country, but they keep judging and comparing themselves using the values they had in their country of origin.

For some, this is a good thing, as it keeps them alive and sane. Having a platform where you are validated according to what you know is a creative way of surviving in a "hostile" environment where, even if you speak the language so that you can function, it is still difficult to understand the underlying values.

Have you ever thought about the invisible luggage that you carried from your country of origin to the adoptive one? Is it easy to find it within yourself?

Where Are You Coming From?

Since you moved to Norway, how many of you have heard this question more times than you want to count? I hear it quite often: "Where are you coming from, really?"

It is a question that us foreigners in Norway will get all our lives. If it is a comfort, Norwegians get it too from their fellows. In Norway, when people move, it is important to keep the dialect they'd learned as they grew up on an island, on a mountain, in a harbor. Dialects vary from town to town and from village to village, even from valley to valley and fjord to fjord. Not uncommon though. There are countries where we meet the same phenomena: Papua New Guinea has 839 first languages.

It is also because, I was told, that quite many Norwegians are interested in dialects and the way the language has developed in different regions. It is also a safe conversation topic.

My impression is that when Norwegians meet a new person, they notice the obvious, the way people speak, and ask where they come from. The intention behind the question is to be nice. It is their curiosity about the new person, and the interest to, maybe, find a new potential friend. If they find out where the stranger comes from, they hope to discover that maybe they had been there, maybe they know someone in the area, maybe they have an experience regarding that place. It means that they want to make the stranger feel welcomed and included.

It is a question, easy to answer, but it does not always bring the feeling intended by the Norwegian asking. They would not know that the person they ask might feel tired of hearing the question repeatedly.

For instance, working at the institution where I spent far more years than I want to count, a guy asked me one day, again, where I came from, and if I were there for a holiday. He was well-intentioned, but he'd asked me this question at least six times over the past three years. Other colleagues ask me this question at least once or twice a year. Well, some may skip the part with where I come from, but another recurrent question is if I am going to travel "home" for my holiday. I have lived in this country almost two decades, yet the time perspective does not fall right for some people, even if they have known me for a long time. Remember the story you read a couple of chapters back about "time comes?" It is the same thing. In my experience, time is irrelevant in this country.

I live in the countryside, so I do "travel" home every single day, and I cannot help answering with this particular detail. They start smiling, get the point, and try to make an excuse, mentioning what "home" means to them—my birth country, the place where I was born and raised.

Even if I do understand that the intention is good, it still annoys me a little. However, the irritation is slowly diminishing in intensity as I spend more time here. I guess I will keep getting these questions indefinitely and from the same people. I am looking at this phenomenon as being my "patience" trial, along with waiting for people to make decisions, to come to conclusions, or to understand new ideas.

How Do You Make Norwegian friends?

It is not easy to make friends among North Norwegians; and yet, it is not impossible. Do not let yourself be scared about the icy expressionless faces. Behind that Ice Wall many of them put up, you can find volcanoes of feelings. All you need to do is to be patient until the ice melts. After that, you'll be surrounded by it as well. Then, you may find out that it is not easy to break out of it.

The key to making friends in Norway is "common interests." This means that you should have some hobbies and find a group of people you can practice them together with. You'll have lots to talk about on that subject. Therefore, it will not be weird for Norwegians who do not ask personal questions, not wanting to intrude as this can be considered impolite. It depends on who you are talking to.

Another thing you can do is to volunteer in various organizations. Find a cause or hobby that you are interested in: poverty, environment, politics, women issues, knitting, singing in a choir, dancing, climbing mountains, parachuting, ice skating, skiing, etc. Find a club or an organization (or more, if you have the time and energy) that deals with precisely that. Join for the activities they have, and you'll get to meet whoever is there. You can find more information on frivilig.no. Just type the city you live in and see what's available there and what is needed to participate.

Each neighborhood or complex of houses or apartment buildings has a board managing it and taking care of the buildings. All that is volunteer work. Join the one that represents the building you live in. It is an excellent way to learn how volunteer organizations work and get to know the people there. They have meetings at least once a month. That is a good opportunity to meet them often enough, so people there have a chance to get to know you.

Making friends in Norway also depends a lot if you came to Norway alone or together with your family (spouse/children). I have noticed that if people come together with their spouses and do not have children, they tend to stick together and not go many places to meet people. It is a behavior which doesn't help them learn the language either.

Couples who have children can make friends easier through their children. They meet other parents at kindergarten and school and extra school activities their children join. If you are good with children yourself and offer to take care of Norwegian children, then you'll be popular, because lots of parents need breaks and time for themselves. And, if you took care of other people's children for some time, the parents would also take care of your children from time to time. It's a nice exchange that allows you to get to know people. Children and school activities are also a great subject to talk about.

When you have a job, you can see if your colleagues are open to making new acquaintances and, eventually, new friendships. Some may be, some not. It will help you a lot if you speak about your interests and hobbies. They will know what you like; and if they have the same interests, they will invite you to talk more about it. You can also make dinner for your colleagues and invite them home. However, do not overdo it and make too many dishes. Just make a simple dinner with one dish and dessert and coffee and drinks. If you overwhelm them with a far-too-rich dinner, you risk scaring them; and they may not invite you back, and they are not going to come again if you ask them again.

If you find out that you cannot break through to your work colleagues, the best thing is to find things to do on your own first. Find other foreigners who perhaps have been in your town longer than you and can advise you where to go and what to do. There are many Facebook groups for foreigners. Just ask who is from the town you live in and see if they want to meet. Remember that friends who are also foreigners are better than no friends at all. If you are determined and show up also in places where Norwegians meet, you will find the right people for you.

It is difficult for Norwegian adults to make new friends in a new place as well. In my experience, from people I know, it took about ten years to make new friends among Norwegians in the new town. And the friends they made were also people who were new in town. This is because many Norwegians do not believe in "friends on the way;" they believe in friends for life. This is why, even if they live in a different town than the one they grew up in, they can still say that they only have one friend or a handful, and those are the buddies from primary school and high school. They do not call people "friend" very easily, and this might stem from them becoming accustomed to people coming and leaving. Therefore, if they are not sure that you'll stick around, they may not want to invest in your friendship. You'll be leaving anyway, so what's the point?

If you come as a student, you're okay because student life is always very social. At the same time, be careful not to socialize solely with international students. Join the cafeterias and the clubs' Norwegian students attend, so you'll also get to meet them. If they are freshmen, they are just as alone as you are in their first year, and they are just forming groups of friends. You have a good chance of becoming a part of those groups. This will be worthwhile if you decide to stay in Norway after finishing your studies. Otherwise, you may find yourself alone when all your international friends have left, and you stayed behind. You will need to start all over again in this friend-making process.

An important detail to keep in mind is that student cafeterias do not require you to buy food there. Student food prices, unfortunately, are not student-friendly in Norway. You can bring your own food like many Norwegian students do. The famous "matpakke" we all learn about when we move to Norway will allow you to be together with Norwegian students, even if your foreign student budget does not allow you to buy the food from the cafeteria.

I hope this gave you some ideas about how to meet Norwegians, even if they are not going to call you "friend" very quickly. If you are present in their lives, if they see you often enough, they will learn that you are also part of the community and may become friendly towards you with time. Remember that time "comes" in Norway.

Why Do Some Norwegians Not Invite You Home for Dinner?

If you already live in Norway, perhaps you've experienced that most Norwegians are very fond of food. Norwegians ask about food from other countries, especially in language courses. It is something they consider essential to being able to speak in Norwegian: food.

At the same time, food sharing has a very different meaning for Norwegians. Even if they enjoy it, many of them consider it "fuel"—something that our body needs to keep us going. You may have noticed that if you are familiar with "matpakke." It is simple, mostly bread and cheese, and just enough to keep the blood sugar in shape.

The fashion of food has increased in Norway in the past ten to fifteen years since people started to travel more. The Internet helps people to see more of what food means in the world, too.

When I moved to Norway, I could not find a proper place to have lunch. The few restaurants in town were open for dinner, which was very expensive for a student like me. Lunch places flourished only after 2010, and I could enjoy a proper European lunch or breakfast.

You may also have noticed that Norwegians feel better if they are out to eat together with you instead of inviting you home. Because they like their homes so much, they consider them a bit "sacred," and not everybody gets to come and visit. I admire and have begun to practice the same approach after understanding this way of thinking.

We foreigners have a tradition to make rich meals for our guests. We often spend much more on food than we can afford because this is how it was in our home countries: honor the guests with more food than they can eat, and with absolutely no regard to their health, or allergies, or even if they are hungry or not.

In my experience and from conversations with Norwegians, I have found out that this kind of dinner can be overwhelming. Why? Because it raises the bar of hospitality very high, and many think that they will never be able to return the favor. As a result, they won't invite you back. People can be afraid that they are not going to match the standards. They think both of their own cooking skills and the money they should spend on that much food, as well as the necessity of spending that much. What's in it for them? How important are you to them?

If they bring a dish, at the end of the evening, many of them are going to take the rest of the dish. It's a reasonable thing to do since they are careful about their budget. But, of course, some people don't care as much. You may notice that those who do not care are very young and grew up with things delivered to them "on a silver plate," as many Norwegian grown-ups say, even if that is their doing because they have raised them that way.

Do not be surprised if you invite Norwegians to dinner and they do not invite you back.

For many of them, dinner is not about the food, as it can be in many other countries. Instead, the dinner is about getting to know each other: people spending time together, mostly around the coffee and tea, and of course, some wine.

I remember my very first time in the place I live. I was lucky enough to be invited to dinner by my neighbors more than once. I used to leave just after the meal because I did not want to be rude by taking too much of their time and making too much use of their hospitality.

At that time, I did not know that leaving just after dinner was rude on my part. They assumed that I was not interested enough in them as people to spend time with them. I was not giving them enough time (and the courage of a couple of glasses of wine) to get to know me.

This is also why they may prefer to meet you out, in a pub or a coffee shop. Each person pays for themself, and the unwritten deal is that "we meet to get to know each other, and we are both willing to pay time and money to do so." This way, both parties know that they are not taken advantage of, and they are respected as human beings and not because they pay for the consumption. There is also a phrase they use when they like you, "Perhaps we should have a coffee together," and then you don't hear anything from them. This is because they don't really mean to have that coffee with you. At the same time, you are interesting enough to them, so at least they could think about spending time in a coffee shop with you. It is a way of saying, "I like you."

I hope this chapter has helped put aside some expectations about people's dinner habits in this country.

Top Secret

"They're supposed to understand!"

I hear this affirmation often. There are things that we are supposed to understand, even if never explained. As foreigners in another country, we are expected to understand much more than we can think of, in the first place. Yet, we have been playing the game of figuring things out since we've been born. It is not necessary that our parents managed to explain everything to us, so we had to figure things out and interpret body language or silence. It is pretty much the same when we move to another country. We learn to "walk" again, "to speak" again, and "to understand" again... a new life in a new system.

Yet, just like everything else, it is not easy to understand many things. For instance, what to do and not do in a particular environment or what to say and not to say in a meeting.

We get a new job, or we volunteer in an organization, and we are in a meeting. We react the way we learned to react in our country of origin, and we say something. Suddenly the facial expressions of the people in the meeting change and the atmosphere becomes different or strange, or tense, or weird. We do not know what we've said nor what happened.

I think everybody has experienced this at some point, but nobody is able to explain what happened and why he or she reacted in a certain way. Is there an unwritten and unspoken rule, which says "we do not speak about that," whatever "that" is? How are we supposed to know if nobody speaks about it, and nobody explains it? I wondered and have been curious about this phenomenon for quite some years now.

Recently, I've had visitors from warmer corners of the world. People who never experienced snow or cold and never had to think about "personal space." Being together with my guests, suddenly part of the answer to the "they're supposed to understand" dilemma came to me, with the awareness over how "Norwegian" I have become.

I've heard questions about how to make fire, or why the cold feels so cold, or why you cannot see the Northern Lights all the time, or why Norway is a monarchy. I listened to frustrations about the dark which was too dark at night. I heard way too much personal information, which I could have happily lived without knowing from a person I had never seen before.

I have also been asked questions just as personal, with the excuse: "I have told you my story, now you have to tell me yours." I didn't ask to hear the story in the first place, so I didn't share mine. I shared what felt natural to the conversation, as I perceived the question as being too direct from a person I had never seen in my life. If I accepted an extra guest in my house, it didn't mean that I had agreed to necessarily connect, at least not in that way.

My guests had been raised and lived in a culture where all these things were permitted and natural. It was difficult to understand why it would be different here, in Norway. In those moments of conversation and explanations, the sentence "you're supposed to understand" crossed my mind, and I realized how difficult it can be to understand something you have never experienced before. It was for me, and still is sometimes, and it is for many other people. Even if I explained that it wasn't how people connected in Norway, my guests still found it hard to understand. In Norway, it takes time to know a person a little bit, and even more time until you hear their life story. Here, life stories are precious and not shared with a stranger on the first day. Yet this is not the case in other cultures nor for the authors who write biographies.

To connect can also mean just being together, even if not speaking; but silence can be a challenge for people from countries where silence between people feels strange and uncomfortable. Personal space and personal story—we're supposed to understand and to know when we can cross boundaries in personal space and when we share personal stories. However, it is not easy to read when you do not know the culture you walked into and you do not get the underlying secrets. Not even the locals know how to discuss these issues, either because it may be something emotionally challenging to speak about or because there was simply never a need to speak of a particular issue. They haven't yet found good expressions they can use, and it will take a while before they will feel comfortable to speak the unspoken.

I chose to speak because, coming from outside and looking at the society, it is easier for me to see. It is like looking into the mirror. When we look at ourselves every day, we stop noticing the way we look and the way we grow old. We do not see ourselves. Yet, other people can notice better, because they look at us longer and better than we do. The same is true with cultures. When one has been living inside a group for many years and knows the rules and the behaviors by heart, they do not need to be spoken.

But if the group finds it is necessary to take in and accept people from outside, the process of mixing and explaining the unwritten rules is not going to be easy. I like to believe that this book will help a little.

Elections

I don't know about you, but I am not political. Yet, I have recently been to a seminar where young politicians discussed why Norwegian citizens with foreign backgrounds are not keen on voting. The Central Bureau for Statistics in Norway (SSB) shows that in 2017, only about half of them have voted for a new Parliament. It sounded interesting since Multiculturalism is my thing, and I decided to go.

Why do people with foreign backgrounds not vote?

Because people do not understand the political system in Norway.

Because people do not speak nor read Norwegian, and all of the information required to learn is only in Norwegian.

Because politics were disappointing in their country of origin, and immigrants take that feeling with them and don't trust Norwegian politicians either.

Because people are not interested in politics at all; they are just interested in the paycheck they get at their jobs.

I am sure each of those people who did not vote in 2017 had their reason. And that is okay.

I don't know if you can vote; but if you can, Google can help you find more information in English. In such a small country, with such a small number of people, YOU can make a difference if you vote.

If you are interested in politics and think it is fun, you can join the team of your favorite political party in your local town, even if you don't speak Norwegian. It will help you get to know people, learn the language better, even make friends, and get those references you need to apply for a job if you don't have one already. Politics is a hobby, and the shared interest brings people together.

Use the opportunity to influence by being there, and to translate their message, at least in English. This way, they can have the opportunity to get more votes. Your presence there, your knowledge, and your way of thinking can make a difference in how they are building their strategy, as well as help them see that there are many foreigners in this country who can contribute.

At the seminar I was telling you about earlier, six young politicians spoke about a multicultural Norway. My question was if they had any close friends with immigrant backgrounds. Two out of six raised their hands. The other four's facial expressions and many other people in the audience were very surprised by this question. It seems that a multicultural Norway did not involve their personal lives. Multiculturalism was just part of a speech until they heard that question.

The following discussion was interesting. It made them think, and I am sure they went home with a different idea about what it means to be "multicultural." It means to have at least one friend from another country; it means to invite them home for dinner; it means to spend time with non-Norwegians.

I am not political and yet I think I made a difference that evening. You can do the same, just by being present at events and gatherings and by being curious and asking questions. You won't change things overnight; but if you can change their course just half a millimeter, that can mean a lot in the long run.

Part 3

Holidays

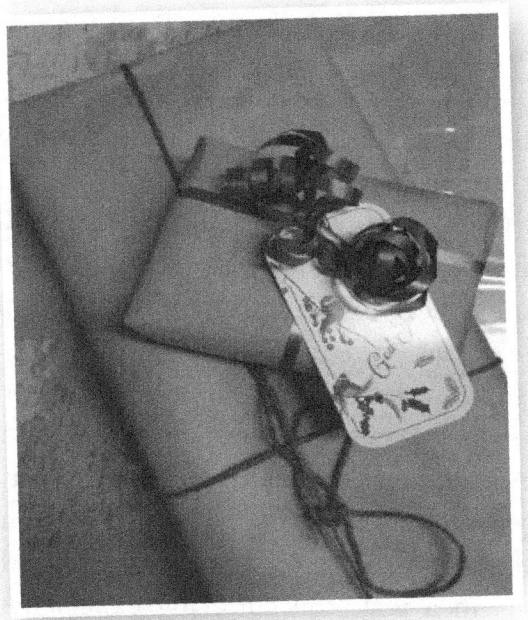

Going Skiing for Easter

Easter is a Christian tradition which marks the sacrifice Jesus made for humanity and his resurrection.

In the Christian world familiar to me (Greek orthodox and catholic), these days are preceded by long weeks of fasting, when you're supposed to be vegan or vegetarian. This means you are not supposed to eat any animal or milk products. Other churches may have rules about refraining from watching TV several weeks before Easter, or refraining from dancing, listening to music, or having sex. As if every single soul should relive, in a way, the suffering experienced by Jesus. All this physical penance concludes with a confession in church; and, if you've been good, the priest gives you the Communion. Thereafter, people sacrifice lambs for the grill and prepare loads of food to celebrate the Resurrection.

Talking to my family or my friends from Southern Europe who belong either to the Greek orthodox church or the Catholic one, I often get asked what people do to celebrate Easter in Norway. "Have you been fasting?" or "Are you going to church on Easter night?" or "Have you painted eggs?" Of course, some of them might get a bit shocked when I say that I do none of this. Although, I do like to paint eggs sometimes, but not every Easter.

Easter in Norway is celebrated with time off work. I think it is one of the few countries in the world where people are free from Wednesday at lunchtime until Monday. Five and one-half days off for Easter. Work starts again the Tuesday after Resurrection. Many people take a whole week off for Easter holiday (the "Silent/Quiet Week"), and it is the most natural and common thing to do. (Interestingly, Easter is not as big of a holiday as Christmas is. Celebrating the Birth of Christ is more important than celebrating his death, even if it is followed by his resurrection.)

At Easter, people stick together, and many Norwegians go to their cabins in the mountains. If they don't have a cabin, they go visit people who have one, or they go and rent one. There, they enjoy skiing and being outside in the sunshine, if there is any. There is absolutely no problem with grilling outside and having a good time building benches in snow, and special places where the atmosphere can be cozy, even if it's cold.

The point is that people disappear from towns. For foreigners who didn't manage to grasp yet how this tradition manifests itself at Easter, it seems very strange and feels very lonely; shops are closed, no entertainment is open, and there is absolutely nothing to do, unless you go to the mountain.

Actually, The Central Bureau of Statistics in Norway (SSB) reports that per 2021, there were about 441,000 cabin owners in Norway. So, where all the other Norwegians (up to 5.5 million now) go, it is inexplicable for people from outside.

So at Easter, I can choose to go skiing (haven't skied in a while now) and to eat oranges and "kvikk lunsj" chocolate. This is pretty much the tradition here. In the two decades I've been here, I can count on one hand the number of people who have mentioned fasting or going to church at Easter. I also have a difficult time explaining fasting. It is something difficult to understand for some (especially elderly) Norwegians. Why would anyone willingly choose to be vegan for forty days?

Some people find veganism difficult to understand in general. I remember being on a trip to Athens in 2013 with a few more grown-up people interested in antique history. We had quite a few meals together, and I usually chose a vegan dish. In Greece, vegetables have taste. They are fresh and the vegan cuisine is just much more varied than in Norway. I enjoyed every salad, every green bean, potato, the beautiful aubergines, and dolmas. I was in heaven. Yet, every time I would tell the waiter I wanted a meat-free dish, my dinner companions asked if I had given up eating meat altogether. Those particular people I was with at that time could not understand why I would not eat meat for breakfast, lunch, and dinner. On my part, it was a very weird thing to do; but otherwise, I was a nice lady (hyggelig dame).

Fasting, being vegan or vegetarian, even for a short while, was not very common in Norway at the time (ca 10 years ago). Yet, in the past few years, I've met people with this lifestyle. Now there is even a Facebook group for the people in my town, with up to 1,000 members currently (2021). The group is called Tromsø

Vegan / Veganere I Tromsø. The language in the group was English in the beginning, but now I see it mixed with Norwegian, which tells me something: There is a generation shift.

My impression is that for the Norwegians I know, the idea of being kind to each other is more common than Easter fasting. Being kind is promoted all days of the year and not only for short holiday periods. I like to believe that the same idea stands behind all the days off one can have at Easter or Christmas. If people have time to rest, to spend time together, and eat well, it is much more likely that they will also be nicer to each other, too.

It doesn't mean that absolutely everything goes well between family members, friends, and neighbors. Yet, many choose to let things be or to behave as if the conflicts and misunderstandings do not exist.

Many people read books at Easter because there is another tradition as well—that of reading crime novels at Easter.

It is called "Påskekrim." The tradition of reading detective books at Easter time started in 1923 with Nordahl Grieg and Nils Lie, two poor writers with no money. They needed to earn something, and they put their heads together and published the novel *Bergen's Train was Robbed Last Night* (Bergenstoget plyndret i natt) under the name Jonathan Jerv.

The title was a huge success because people thought it was true when they saw the newspaper advertisement. They didn't have the patience to read the whole article, talking about a book release. Ever since, Norwegians look forward to reading crime books at Easter, and the phenomenon has spread over the years.

Crime is easy to read and accessible to all people. As many other styles, it allows identifying with characters; at the same time, it also offers the thrill of solving a puzzle. It draws the reader in and allows them to experience some sides of themselves that cannot be experienced in everyday life. It is also a very good conversation topic for when people meet. It's neutral, and it is better to gossip about some fictitious evil characters than about real people.

I assume Norwegians like crime because the country is very safe and stable economically and has been like this for decades. One way for people to experience bad stuff is in novels. As I said, this last paragraph is my assumption, and I cannot be sure if it is valid for each Norwegian who reads this genre.

Another personal assumption is that perhaps in countries where people experience bad stuff in everyday life and are poorly treated by others and misbehave, they do not want to read the same things in books. They would prefer to read beautiful and philosophical stuff, which is not experienced in their real life. I have no idea if this is true.

Happy May 17th

The 17th of May is Norwegian National day. In 1814 on this day, the Norwegian Constitution was signed. It is a National Holiday; therefore, everybody is free of work and school. Exceptions are people who need to be on duty: nurses, firefighters, police, etc.

This day is celebrated everywhere in Norway, from small villages to big towns. It is a happy day, especially for children, as they get to have all the hotdogs and ice cream they can eat. One could say that this is how the love for their nation and their country is fed to people. It seems to be an event which is planting the foundation of Norwegian democracy in people's minds.

The parents might not be as happy since they have a lot to prepare: the national costumes for those who have them and beautiful clothes for those who don't have national costumes. At the same time, they don't really have a choice if children are involved. They cannot risk the social life of children by not letting them get involved in this school activity. Nobody wants to be left out or pushed out of their groups because they did not experience the same things together.

National costumes are quite expensive to buy. Young teenagers get them as presents for their confirmation when they reach fourteen years old. They can be inherited from family members, or all the family donates money to buy one. Sometimes, family members decide to make it themselves if they are good at tailoring, embroidery and sewing.

In towns, the municipality helps with organizing the parade on the main streets and everybody gets to take part in the parade. Everybody gets access to a program for the day, so people know what time of the day they have to join the show: from kindergarten children to children who go to school or high school. Those who are in the last year of high school have a special parade, called Russetog, where they can manifest as much crazy behavior as they possibly can. The parades start a few days before May 17th and culminate with the big ceremony on this day. The teenagers get to dress up in special uniforms or costumes and then drive buses or cars bought and painted especially for the occasion. This bus/car driving is quite a big deal, and these vehicles can also cost a lot of money. But never mind that, only once in a lifetime one gets to be Russ. With this occasion, some of the teenagers may also get drunk. It is a forbidden fruit they get to taste at this time in their lives, and they use this chance to try it. They're not allowed to buy any alcohol until the age of eighteen, but this rule doesn't stop them from asking older friends to do them favors. A good illustration of teenage life can be found in the movie "Skam" (Shame).

Nonprofit organizations have their time in the parade as well when they get to show what they stand for and the causes they work for or promote.

Ordinary citizens dress up and have their place in the parade too. It is a big "people party." For some Norwegians, the National Day is more important than Christmas Day. In North Norway, where I live, spring is around the corner and the snow has just melted. The spiked tires are replaced with summer tires, and everybody and everything is involved in cleaning and washing the town, the yards, the houses, for this big day.

The flags come out to make buildings pretty and to mark the day.

May 17th is also a day when people meet for breakfast. In my experience, it is not customary to gather in meetings for this meal, except at work. But on this day, it's an exception and people allow themselves to drink alcohol all day, beginning at breakfast time. It is a day of celebration, so why not? It is important to dress up for the occasion, have a nice meal and be together with family, friends, and the rest of the town.

In small places, people gather around schools. They bake cakes at home and bring them to school, make coffee, and have a little parade for the village.

A couple of years ago, there was a big debate in the media about the immigrants participating at the parade; whether they should be allowed to wave the flag of their country of origin, or the Norwegian flag. The discussion also brought up the issue of whether or not Norwegians approve of people with a different skin color than the traditional Nordic Blond wearing the Traditional Norwegian Costume or waving the Norwegian flag. I have no idea if the discussion had a conclusion, but it certainly brought forward some critical issues the country's politicians are dealing with right now.

These past years, we were dealing with the Corona virus and gatherings were forbidden.

Writing and revising this chapter, I realized why this kind of celebration can be strange for immigrants and visitors from other countries. It is because we don't see any display of military power as we are used to in our birthlands.

Many national days have to do with independence-making wars or some sort of fights. Therefore, these days are marked by parades with soldiers and guns so people can be reminded how independence was achieved.

In Norway, there has been peace for a long time. Celebrating the ground rules of Norwegian democracy, where people are supposed to be equal and share the same rights and duties, seems the natural thing to do here.

Happy 17th of May!

July and Summer Holiday in North Norway

Once upon a time, far, far North, there was a country where everything was set in "power save" mode, if not completely "shut down" for an entire month: July. This month, almost everybody takes a holiday and rests.

Except for grocery stores, all shops close at 16:00, perhaps 18:00 (in Oslo). In offices, you will only find replacements, who are young people in charge of the summer activity. Many of them are there with the sole task of smiling at you and telling you to come back in August. In many places, if one person in charge of an important project is on holiday, then the entire activity of the project is stopped until the person in charge comes back.

A couple years ago, a friend from the South visited me in July, and I took her to a very famous place here, in North Norway, called Sommarøy.

It was a very beautiful, sunny summer day. We walked on the white beach, and we could get close to the holiday houses strategically placed on the shore. We could look inside to see how cozy they were but empty because in July, pretty much everything is "dead." We had dinner at the restaurant in the village's hotel where we were the only guests. Nevertheless, the salmon dish was exquisite. Perhaps because there were so few customers, the chef took extra time and care to prepare it.

Yes, July is the summer holiday for most Norwegians. The Unions have fought hard to get workers the right to have a holiday, preferably three weeks in a row, if not four. Norwegian researchers have concluded that a working human body needs a three-week break to rebuild itself. Only in the fourth week can one say that the human body and mind are rested and can be productive again. Anyway, three weeks in a row is recommended by doctors; and employers are forced by law to give this time to their employees.

Another reason is that, in July, children are on holiday from school. In Norway, it is not common to just shuffle your kids off to their grandparents and leave them there for the summer while the parents go away on holiday by themselves. Many parents take care of their children pretty much on their own (without much help from grandparents), and they stay home with the children during summer; or they travel away with them, as a family. It is called "quality time." Grandparents have just as much right to have a holiday as everybody else. There is a saying among retired people which is often accompanied by a smile: "I'm retired, I have no time." This is also because at this age, many of them have both the time and the money to do the things they had wanted but had never had time or money to do when they were younger.

Location preferences for holidays vary. Some would go and spend time at their cottages in the mountains. Doing small jobs around the cabin like carpentry, painting, wood sawing or cutting grass are typically summer holiday activities considered relaxing. The time is also relaxing when garnished with good food, wine or beer, and no alarm to wake you up. Midnight Sun is also a detail, which contributes to forgetting the time and messing up the nights and days. The Polar Day lasts for about three months.

Others take the caravan and travel around. During summer, driving in North Norway can be challenging as there are so many caravans one meets on the road. You can tell if they know the road or not by watching how fast they drive through the curvy roads between the fjords. The speed limit is 90 km per hour, but a foreigner is more likely to drive 70 km per hour. It is not fun being stuck behind them, especially when you know the road like the back of your palm, and you want to hurry home.

There are also quite a few hitchhikers along the roads. This is a way some foreigners choose to spend a summer holiday as well. Hitchhiking around North Scandinavia, while there is 24/7 light and Midnight Sun, can be an experience; and you don't have to be afraid of the dark.

I like to believe that I do my share of picking up hitchhikers for the short distance I drive on the main road. I find it a good way to get in touch with the rest of the world. From what they say, it is mostly foreigners who pick them up. Very seldom, or never, Norwegians. I am not surprised. If it is July, most Norwegians are on holiday, in other places on the planet, most likely "Syden" or "The South," in a country with a beach. Many Norwegians call "Syden" all countries in Europe, with or without a sea opening. This is because the only places they want to visit are those with a beach where they can bathe in the sun. This is considered the perfect holiday for most of them, of course garnished with good, cheap food, and especially wine or other alcoholic beverages they can get almost for free. In fact, in "Syden," water bottles are more expensive than wine bottles. So, why not enjoy the cheap wine?

If you live in North Norway, as I do, wanting to go to "Syden" is also a necessity, especially because we experience the polar night, and we do not have sunlight for almost four months during the winter; and then, in the summer, there is no guarantee that there is going to be sunshine at all. Often, we experience a Green Winter with a lot of clouds and a lot of rain. The temperatures can be very low, close to zero during the night, and not much above during the day; and we miss the Sun and the real Summer, with at least 20 degrees Celsius. Most of us want to secure at least a few days of sun, for health's sake, during this time in July. We cannot rely on the weather. In August, it is already autumn, and a new working year starts.

People from abroad are not used to this lifestyle, where your employer is forced to give you a three-week holiday during "fellesferie" which means "holiday for everybody." It is referring to July when everybody takes time off at the same time. I have heard comments about how much "business" and money Norway is losing due to this rule. Maybe, but this rule also means respect for people. However, it is true that many still work during the summer holiday. Mostly in cleaning, grocery stores, hospitals, and elderly houses where students work, and many foreigners, too. But the tempo can be lower and, of course, influenced by the weather.

The North Norwegian Cabin Trip

If you've been mingling with Norwegians in the last few years, perhaps you have noticed that many of them have both a house and a cabin. If they don't own the cabin themselves, someone in their family does. It is either by the sea or by the mountain, or both, since these sceneries make the charm of nature in Norway. Some of the cabins are almost as fancy as a house in town with all the comfort needed, including TV and Internet. Others do not have water; or if they have water, they do not have electricity or the other way around; or they lack both.

Cabin trips are trendy among Norwegians. Why? Because at the cabin, they can change the scenery. They can relax without thinking of the time passing or of other people. There they can be only with the people they choose to be. Many of them have these cabins as family projects. To repair, to paint, to do some gardening, just for fun. I do understand it because I chose to live at the cabin all year round. Mine has all the comforts.

In the area I live, there are many cabins with no water or without electricity, or, as I mentioned before, without both. Therefore, I asked some friends why they would bother to have a cabin with no water and electricity. They answered that this is an excellent way to remind themselves how it was in the old days—how their great grandparents lived. They would enjoy the food and coffee made on a bonfire, the smell of smoke, and even the fact that they won't have to worry about washing for a couple of days. The quick bath taken in the cold mountain river or in the sea was much more fun. When they return home and have access again to the comfort of electricity and running water, they can be even more grateful for what they have.

I remember one of my Norwegian colleagues I met while studying. He used to go out for lunch on campus, only wearing a sweater, even if it was freezing outside, especially in the winter. When we asked him why he would do that, he answered, "I like the feeling of my body waking up when I get outside; and then, when I get back inside, I enjoy the feeling of warmth and coziness. It makes me appreciate the comfort I am lucky to have here and all the resources we are provided here on Campus." It was an honest and straightforward answer which, for me, was pointing to his gratitude for what he had. He didn't want to take for granted a warm room and comfort, because he was aware of the fact that not everybody has it. He felt lucky, and so did I.

After some experiences at cabins together with people who became dear to me (and I like to believe I to them), I met other foreigners complaining about being invited to places by Norwegians. Of course, it is a good thing to be invited to the cabin. Yet, they were not given heads up that there would not be water and electricity there. It was expected to be common knowledge, and the guests should know that some lack is normal.

It is a general thing for people to believe that everybody knows what is in their heads, including people from other countries. It isn't easy to imagine that some people may have different experiences when it comes to comfort. Therefore, they could not think that lacking water and electricity for a couple of days may not be FUN for everybody.

There are still many regions in the world where many houses do not have running water. People who grew up in this kind of condition may not appreciate a cabin without this comfort. Bringing water to a household takes a lot of time and energy for these people, in opposition to the idea of fun that some Norwegians have about it.

If you are not sure if you would like to go to the cabin, think twice before you say NO to a Norwegian who invites you. Ask about the cabin's condition and prepare a polite answer in case you decide that the trip is not for you. Liking or not liking to go to the cabin may have to do with the experiences you have from your country of origin when it comes to the comfort of electricity, water, or walking distance.

Some of these cabins may be at a considerable distance from the road. Then you may need to walk up the mountain, carrying all the things you need for your stay, including water tanks. Many Norwegians also prefer physical bodily restraint since moving and doing all kinds of sports is very popular. If something is allowed to be bragged about, it is physical resilience and sports.

It is also good to remember that some Norwegians who are generous enough to invite strangers to their cabins may have not traveled too much. Therefore, they might not have that much knowledge of the previous living conditions of their guests unless the guests have shared their story precisely. At the same time, a trip to the cabin can be an excellent time to "glue" the relationship. The time spent together, agreeing or disagreeing on small things around making dinner and coffee and fire, add to the quality of the relationship you may build together. Relationships are not easy, no matter where you are!

Potato Holiday

If you are a parent living in Norway and you have kids in school, you'll notice they have a week of holiday in October.

Yet, this week of holiday in the autumn varies from county to county. This means that children from the South of Norway do not have this holiday at the same time as children from North Norway. This may seem strange because it does not seem to fit any national education plan, yet people who work in education have adjusted the subject's progression through the year by taking this holiday into account.

This holiday, in the middle of October, has to do with nature and harvesting and is known as the "Potato Holiday."

Why?

Before 1969 when Norway discovered oil, and even some good years after that, people were poor; they needed all the labor they could get in the autumn for the harvest.

The time good for gathering the growth of soil just before winter is short, and the weather is moody. Therefore, parents needed their children to help pick up the vegetables (potatoes, carrots, cabbage) before the frostbite.

Autumn holiday is something that exists in many countries, and it has to do with harvesting. However, it is placed at different times in different counties during September and October, according to the climate in each country.

Did you have a "Potato Holiday" in your country? If yes, when was it placed? What did you used to do as a kid at that time?

Home for Christmas

The classic cliché title. There are so many clichés when it comes to Christmas and the way we celebrate it. We construct an ideal picture about the way we need to celebrate it, and some people literally break their necks so they can make it happen. It's as if being together with loved ones matters only for one day or a couple of days, and not for the rest of the year.

We repeatedly hear the same questions from friends, colleagues, and acquaintances: "What are you going to do for Christmas?" "Are you going home?" "What are you going to have for Christmas dinner?"

My experience is that each of us has a Christmas picture in our head. When we ask others what they do for Christmas, we actually wish to tell what the picture in our head looks like. We ask, so we get to be asked in return. I rarely meet people genuinely interested in what

I do for Christmas. It is mostly small talk, just a way to pass the time and perhaps to look polite. Yet, small talk can be important sometimes, too.

As Norwegians surround me every day, of course the Norwegian Christmas traditions come up. It seems that when you don't present a picture similar to theirs when talking about Christmas celebrations, it shakes their world. Sometimes, I have some work to do, so I am going to spend some time working. Once, a Norwegian interlocutor asked, "What kind of job do you have, if you have to work during Christmas?"

I know plenty of Norwegian people who work during holidays (nurses, doctors, fire-fighters, policemen, etc.), yet it seems that it is not the right picture to present, even if it is true. The person did not wait for my answer and continued to tell me that they are going to be together with family, accidentally in the same area as where I live. "Well, drop by for a cup of coffee, if you get the chance," I offered. The person stopped for a moment, looked at me for the first time during the conversation, and answered with a confused expression on their face, "I don't think so. Christmas is family, sooo much family." The conversation mainly continued with me hearing all about how that person's family was going to celebrate Christmas together. I've heard both good and bad episodes, and less fortunate discussions which come up every year. Nobody talks to each other the rest of the year, and of course, the unfinished business comes up repeatedly at the Christmas table. Everybody is on their toes, so that feelings can be spared for Christmas.

My experience with some of the Norwegian people I meet is that many are so afraid of having uncomfortable discussions or confrontations that they end up in uncomfortable situations just as well. How comfortable can it be when you don't say what you mean because you do not want to ruin Christmas? My question is why things aren't discussed in between Christmases, so people won't have to struggle so much on holidays. Some bloggers and trendy magazines have already issued articles titled "How to Keep Peace with the Family on Christmas Holidays" or "How to Tolerate Family at Christmas," and Netflix has a funny mini-series called "Home for Christmas." (You need to know a bit of Norwegian to read the articles, hear the podcast/webinars, or watch the films.)

When I speak about this and the way people want to keep the peace while they are together,

I am also aware of the background I have where people are sharper and more direct, not necessarily afraid to "spice" things up by the way they use language or speak from "their livers," as we say in Norway. I am one of those people, speaking from the liver. Proof of that is also this book. It is not always comfortable either, to act this way; at the same time, my experience is that it is just as uncomfortable not to speak from the liver. It only delays an uncomfortable situation or piles up frustrations, which eventually will pop up somewhere else or at a later Christmas dinner.

Regarding the same Christmas holiday, another Norwegian woman told me that she didn't have any other friends outside her close and extended family. She did not think it was proper for her to have friends that were not from early childhood, or to go into places where she could meet other people. She told me many times that she felt trapped in the family, and that she could not escape. It was painful to hear how sad she was about it, yet she could not get out of the "programming" she received as a child. She is going to spend holidays with family, even if she knows they are not going to be pretty. She is determined to make the imposed commercial picture about how Christmas should be, even if it is going to cost her tears. Even though at the time of the discussion, she had known me for more than thirteen years and shared things with me that she wouldn't tell any of her other friends, she still could not call me her "friend." I am a foreigner, and it was not proper.

Another pattern I've seen in this country is that most couples spend Christmas separately, with their parents, without taking their partner with them. At least not as long as they do not have children. When children appear, the new family makes new traditions. It is as if they still want to be children for as long as possible. There is nothing wrong with that. It's good to be able to be a child no matter what your ID says. Of course, as long as it is nice to be with family. Parents also want to have their children as long as possible. Once I heard one of my colleagues who has children say, "Having your children choosing to live close to you is a luxury." His next comment was, "We cannot say the same thing about your mother." He was absolutely right. My mother has only one child close to her, out of four. (I like Khalil Gibran's poem *About Children* a lot.)

Going back to the children being children as long as they are allowed, I believe that it is easier to keep peace in the family when you don't bring a "stranger" that you've chosen as your life partner, especially if you do not know if you are going to have kids with or marry that person. This uncertainty can last for many years, since a good percentage among the Norwegians I know did not marry; more than half live in partnerships all their lives. It seems that the trends are changing in the last few years, and many young people are choosing to marry after all. I was told that it may also have to do with what people see on TV and internet, wanting the beautiful ritual with a nice ceremony, dress, values, and party, etc.

In my experience, as someone who has moved away from home and lived among "strangers" at quite a young age, I believe you can call family the people you choose yourself, in the place you find yourself, at a certain time in your life. There can be people you've met for the first time, yet the atmosphere around them can be more loving than in any "family." I enjoy the time I have with my blood family when I am with them. Otherwise, the people who are with me at a certain time and place are my "family," and I enjoy their presence regardless of the country and the culture they come from. (After I shared this article with some people, a friend and a good critic took the time to draw my attention over the fact that the saying "home is where your heart is" is also a cliché. Agree, then, this is my cliché, since we live our lives following clichés).

People are not always easy to handle at any time of year, family or not family. How many of us can say that we actually "know" the people in our family very well? We grow, we travel, we change and all this changes the family dynamics. What remains is the image of the old family we had when we were living under the same roof; and either we recreated it or we are together with blood family, by cooking the same meals and cakes and by remembering stories from the old times. If we are not together with a blood family, we do the same by sharing our stories and traditional recipes with the people available to us there and then.

It remains to add that not everyone celebrates Christmas, yet people use the occasion to meet and to be together, not necessarily as family, but as friends.

Have you ever thought about how you would really like to spend Christmas? Apart from the traditions imposed on us by society and commercial trends and consumerism. If you have another picture in mind, what stops you from making it real? Or, to put it differently, which Christmas cliché would you like to live after?

Holiday During Corona

In Spring 2021, I had been visiting my family in a red zone. Red for Norway, because people ruling this country are cautious and prefer to take extra care measures than risk people's health. Therefore, when I came back to Norway, I was in quarantine for nine days.

I arrived in Norway via Torp airport. There was a long queue at passport control, and then we were taken inside a room where we were tested. The test was free of charge and the result came in about fifteen minutes. After that, we were distributed to places of quarantine. For me, it was Scandic Park Hotel in Sandefjord. We were taken there by taxi, that too, free of charge.

The quarantine rules were handed out together with practical information, which included meals. They were supposed to be placed outside our doors at 08:00 for breakfast, 12:00 for lunch, and 18:00 for dinner. They were to be accompanied by a knock on the door, except for breakfast. The staff didn't want to wake us up at 08:00 in the morning if not necessary. I was impressed by the care and respect for people's sleep. We were getting three meals a day and overnight for 500 NOK a day. A good price for Norway and for this significant hotel in the Vestfold area. The room I got was big, with a beautiful view of the park in front of the hotel. Fresh sheets and towels, all clean.

The maids weren't allowed to get into the quarantine rooms for their protection and ours; therefore, we were expected to help with the cleaning if we felt the need. That was logical to me, and it seemed fair for the price as well. With the characteristic smiles and politeness, the staff was helping in any way they could. Most of the quarantine guests would respect the rules and be polite and behave. However, some did not.

Nobody wants to stay in quarantine. *Yet, if this is the case, at least it's better to make a good experience out of it,* I thought.

I have never been to this little town in the South of Norway before. We were allowed to walk outside, which gave me the chance to look around the small city center with cozy houses and crossroads on every corner of the tiny streets.

One afternoon I returned to the hotel from my walk and passed by two of the hotel employees. One man from security and one woman were talking on their way home. The woman complained to her colleague about how some of the quarantine guests picked on her long legs.

"That was not nice," said the man. "Do you want me to do anything about it?"

"No, let them be," she answered, showing the group of men who were walking towards the end of the corridor, inside the hotel. "I just don't understand how they cannot know that this kind of comment is rude." A sad expression crossed her face.

Pity, I was thinking. Perhaps no one told the men (I don't know which country they were from) that this kind of comment is considered "sexual harassment" in Norway and is illegal. This time, they got away. Next time, they may not.

For me, the experience of quarantine was not at all a struggle. On the contrary, I took it as an extra week of holiday. I didn't feel in any way that my liberty was too constrained. Throughout the week, I got some messages on my phone to remind me that I was in quarantine and got one call from the people in charge, mostly to check on me and see if I knew the rules of quarantine.

I was getting food every day, which I didn't have to think of buying and preparing myself. Some shortened, in terms of vegetables, since the good old Norwegian "kost" (cooking) does not include too many of those. However, I knew it was only for a maximum of ten days, and I didn't have to eat what I didn't like.

We were allowed to walk around town and take the typical hikes you can find everywhere around the small towns in Norway. However, we were not allowed to go into the shops or other buildings or visit people in the hotel (if we knew any). I didn't think it was such a terrible constraint. I didn't know anyone, and shops one can find everywhere.

I like walking and hiking and discovered lovely corners of the town that were quite charming. The days I stayed in went on fine since I was determined not to let it ruin my mood. I also had my computer with me, which allowed me to write and work. I would have done that anyway, no matter where I was. And here, even more since I had no care for daily hustle.

At the same time, every time I went in and out of the hotel, I would see and hear angry people. Angry about feeling trapped. Angry about having to pay for the quarantine themselves. Angry about wasted time. Angry about finding out that some of the other guests had tested positive on the seventh day of quarantine and moved to another part of the hotel called "isolation." *It happens everywhere*, I thought. *Nothing is perfect.*

It was not a pretty sight. I was grateful for the time I took to learn to enjoy my own company and look at the full half of the glass instead of the empty one. What could I have solved if I would have gotten angry? Who would have cared, and how would that have changed the situation?

Did I lose time? Yes and no. I still did a lot of stuff and tried another version of the concept of "working remote," which was a good experience. Now I know what it's about in another sense than just having an office at home.

Did I lose money? Yes, on some flight tickets which I booked, thinking that I may get out before I did. One of the reasons would be that the machines that were supposed to analyze the test I took on my seventh day of quarantine broke, and the result was delayed by a day. Since there were so many people testing, that was not a surprise; yet some moments of irritation accompanied it. I am human. And of course, I had paid those 500 NOK a night for nine nights altogether.

I got home safe and sound and, even more importantly, healthy, which allowed me to work and replace the money I "lost." Yet, I do not necessarily consider it "lost." My need to see my family and some few dear friends I hadn't seen since long before the pandemic was more expensive than predicted. Was it worth it? Absolutely. I would not be without it.

If you decide to travel, look thoroughly through the regulations around traveling and the places where you're supposed to do the quarantine. Engage it as an experience rather than as a restriction. Health is essential, and some governments take extra care, like the Norwegian one, which is a positive thing. Yet, one can never be too careful. In the fall of 2021, the pandemic started up again as a result of borders opening during the summer and people traveling again. And soon after Christmas, in 2022, everything went back to normal again. Corona disappeared like a bad dream. It seems we have been in a bubble for almost two years, and now we are out of it; and Corona is regarded as a simple cold.

Soon after, the war in Ukraine started a new global crisis. It seems that times keep being challenging in one way or another.

The End

or

To Be Continued

Thank You Note

First, I am grateful for the experience of being an immigrant in Norway. And from this, I am grateful for all the people I've met and still meet on this journey—people who inspire me every day to write something about how I understand their culture, which I feel how slowly it becomes also mine.

I am grateful for all the other immigrants I've met who, through conversations and their behavior, have confirmed my impressions.

I am grateful for the ladies I meet every month in my book club, who have read my book and given me constructive feedback—gently, with the care and diplomacy that Norwegians are famous for. Thank you, ladies!

I am grateful for my sister, D., who has supported me in the process of making the decision to publish this book.

I am grateful for my colleague, Marit, who took the time to read my book and provided the end note on the back cover. Thank you Marit!

Last and not least, I am grateful to Amanda Johnson and her team for her help with the final steps of producing this book.

Thank you!

Gabriela Sirbu

If you liked what you've read in this book, and you would like to receive more news and articles on the subject of Norwegian culture, you can sign up for my newsletter by accessing this link: https://migrationofemotion.simplero. com/page/144171

Books and authors mentioned in the book, for those who would like to read more.

The 7 Habits of Highly Effective People by Stephen R. Covey

The Growth of Soil by Knut Hamsun

Freakonomics by Steven Levitt and Stephen J. Dubner

Pippi Longstocking by Astrid Lindgren

The Culture Map by Erin Meyer

The Drama of Being a Child by Alice Miller

Kristin Lavransdatter by Sigrid Undset

Norwegian Gender Equality History 1814 – 2013

Gabriela Sirbu is a therapist, speaker, and writer at migrationofemotion.com. She is a former journalist (BA) and has a master's degree in Peace and Conflict Transformation from UiT The Arctic University of Norway and a specialization within practical psychology from the Norwegian Gestalt Institute in Oslo.

Gabriela has been studying, living, and working in Norway for nearly twenty years. Now, among other things, she works as a therapist and consultant and holds seminars and workshops on multicultural communications to help people become aware of how their invisible luggage is influencing their communication patterns, their behavior, and their lives.

Made in the USA
Monee, IL
18 February 2025

75801393R00118